THE DINOSAUR LIBRARY

Great Dinosaur Expeditions and Discoveries
Adventures with the Fossil Hunters

Thom Holmes and Laurie Holmes
Illustrated by Michael William Skrepnick

Series Advisor:
Dr. Peter Dodson
Professor of Veterinary Anatomy and Paleontology,
University of Pennsylvania
and
co-editor of *The Dinosauria,*
the leading reference used by dinosaur scientists

Enslow Publishers, Inc.

40 Industrial Road	PO Box 38
Box 398	Aldershot
Berkeley Heights, NJ 07922	Hants GU12 6BP
USA	UK

http://www.enslow.com

Library of Congress Cataloging-in-Publication Data

Holmes, Thom.
    Great dinosaur expeditions and discoveries: adventures with the fossil hunters /
Thom Holmes and Laurie Holmes.
        p. cm. — (The dinosaur library)
    Summary: Outlines several expeditions by paleontologists hunting for information
about dinosaurs in America, Africa, Canada, Patagonia, and elsewhere.
    Includes bibliographical references and index.
    ISBN 0-7660-2078-9 (hardcover)
    1. Paleontology—Juvenile literature. 2. Dinosaurs—Juvenile literature.
3. Paleontologists—Juvenile literature. [1. Paleontology. 2. Dinosaurs.
3. Paleontologists.] I. Holmes, Laurie. II. Title. III. Series.
QE714.5.H63 2003
560—dc21
                                                    2002153851

Printed in the United States of America

10 9 8 7 6 5 4 3 2 1

To Our Readers: We have done our best to make sure all Internet Addresses in this book were
active and appropriate when we went to press. However, the author and the publisher have
no control over and assume no liability for the material available on those Internet sites or on
other Web sites they may link to. Any comments or suggestions can be sent by e-mail to com-
ments@enslow.com or to the address on the back cover.

Illustration Credits: Michael William Skrepnick

Photo Credits: © 1999 Artville, LLC, pp. 25, 29, 41, 54, 69, 92; Neg. no. 312408,
courtesy the Library, American Museum of Natural History (AMNH), p. 16; Neg.
no. 19508, AMNH, p. 57; Neg. no. 18552, AMNH, p. 60; Neg. no. 18547,
AMNH, p. 64; Neg. no. 410960, AMNH, p. 72; Neg. no. 410944, AMNH,
p. 73; Neg. no. 411014, AMNH, p. 74; Neg. no. 410737, AMNH, p. 77; Neg.
no. 410765, AMNH, p. 78; Neg. no. 410782, AMNH, p. 81; L. Chiappe, pp. 96,
98; © Corel Corporation, pp. 6–7, 53, 82; Glenbow Archives NA-3250-7, p. 62;
Glenbow Archives NA-3250-10, p. 66; Wayne Grady, p. 4 (Thom Holmes); The
Granger Papers Project, p. 43; Shaina Holmes, p. 4 (Laurie Holmes); Thom
Holmes, pp. 14, 28, 40, 68, 91, 94, 101; Library of Congress, p. 17; Museum für
Naturkunde der Humbolt—Universität zu Berlin, pp. 32, 33, 35; Courtesy of the
Peabody Museum of Natural History, Yale University, New Haven, CT, p. 19; Josh
Smith, pp. 44, 51; Michael Tropea, p. 5.

Cover Illustration: Michael William Skrepnick

Cover Photo: Neg. no. 18552, courtesy the Library, American Museum of Natural
History

CONTENTS

ABOUT THE AUTHORS

Thom Holmes is a natural history writer specializing in dinosaur science. He has dug for dinosaurs with leading paleontologists in the United States and South America. He has collaborated with Dr. Peter Dodson on several dinosaur-related projects during the past fifteen years.

Laurie Holmes is a science writer and editor, as well as a reading specialist. It has been her privilege to associate with many of the world's leading dinosaur scientists and artists through her work with Thom. Originally a teacher, she maintains that she is still teaching by writing and editing books for young adults.

On a dig in Patagonia, Thom Holmes holds part of the skull bone of what is currently known as the largest meat-eating dinosaur ever.

Thom Holmes

Laurie Holmes

AUTHORS' NOTE

In writing *The Dinosaur Library*, we enjoyed sharing the knowledge that allows scientists to understand what dinosaurs were really like. The series covers all the suborders of dinosaurs, from the meat-eating theropods, such as *Tyrannosaurus rex*, to the gigantic plant eaters. It also includes the pterosaurs, flying reptiles that lived during the same time as the dinosaurs. We hope you enjoy learning about these fascinating creatures that ruled the earth for 160 million years.

About the Illustrator

Michael William Skrepnick is an established paleo artist with a lifelong interest in dinosaurs. He has worked on newly described dinosaurs with a number of the world's leading paleontologists. His original artworks are found in a number of art collections and reproduced as museum murals, and in popular books, magazines, scientific journals, and television documentaries.  Michael lives and works in Alberta, Canada, close to some of the richest Upper Cretaceous dinosaur fossil localities in the world.

✦ ✦ ✦

Paleo art is a field devoted to the reconstruction and life restoration of long extinct animals and their environments. Since we cannot observe dinosaurs (other than living birds) in nature, we may never truly know their habits, lifestyles, or the color of their skin. In addition, the fossil record provides only a fraction of the remains of a wide diversity of life on earth.

Many fairly complete skeletons of dinosaurs have been unearthed in recent history. Others are represented by as little as a fragment of a single fractured bone, an isolated tooth, or a footprint impressed in once-wet mud. It is still possible to create a reliable portrait of unique, previously unknown creatures, but the accuracy of the art depends on the following:

- The quality and amount of actual skeletal material of the specimen preserved
- Discussion and collaboration with a paleontologist familiar with the fossil material and locality from which it was excavated
- Observation and comparisons to the closest related living forms
- The technical abilities, skill, and disciplined vision of the artist

The resulting artwork can draw the viewer back in time into exotic worlds of the ancient.

CHAPTER 1

PALEONTOLOGY: DISCOVERING LIFE OF THE PAST

What is it like to hunt for dinosaurs? Where are they found? What does it feel like to hold an ancient bone that has not seen the light of day for over 65 million years? These are some of the questions that any student of dinosaurs wants to ask.

The science of dinosaurs begins in the field, where ancient bones are recovered for study. Dinosaur bones have been found on every continent. Parts of North America and Asia, particularly China, are the richest locations for finding dinosaurs. In the United States and China, dinosaur bones are often found close to major cities, highways, and other populated areas. The Rocky Mountain states in America—including Colorado, Utah, Montana, and Wyoming—are famous for

Geographic
Dinosaur

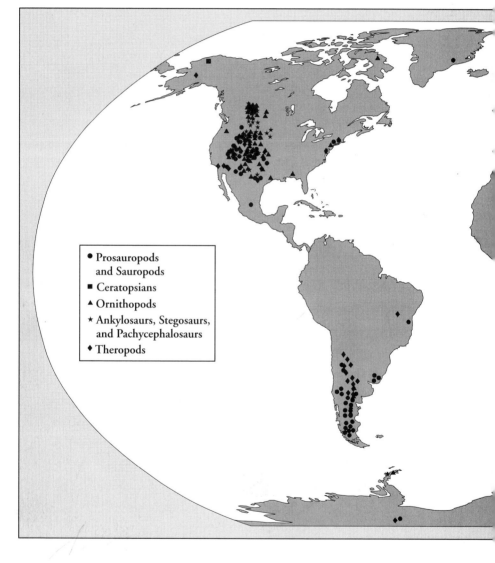

- • Prosauropods
  and Sauropods
- ■ Ceratopsians
- ▲ Ornithopods
- ★ Ankylosaurs, Stegosaurs,
  and Pachycephalosaurs
- ◆ Theropods

Range of Fossils

magnificent dinosaur discoveries. The province of Alberta, Canada, is equally good. In Egypt, the Baharīya Oasis is only 160 miles (260 kilometers) from the bustling city of Cairo. One of the very richest sites in the world is in Liaoning, China. This is an agricultural area only 300 miles (480 kilometers) northeast of the capital, Beijing. Other continents where dinosaur science is booming include South America and Africa.

How does a scientist know where to look for dinosaurs? The first clue is by knowing the age of the exposed land formations in any given part of a continent. Dinosaur bones are found only in sedimentary rocks. These are rocks that were formed gradually over time—sometimes over many millions of years—from the breakdown of older rocks. They are formed in layers on the surface of the earth. The oldest parts of the rock are the lowest layers. It takes a certain amount of time for rock layers to form. Geologists—scientists who study rock formations—can tell how old sedimentary rocks are by their thickness, order, and makeup. When a dead dinosaur was buried by mud or sand, its bones eventually became fossilized while they were trapped inside a sedimentary rock in the making.

Dinosaur bones are found in sedimentary rocks that date from 65 million to about 225 million years ago. The best places to search for dinosaurs are often dry and lacking in thick vegetation. These are sometimes called badlands, where few trees are found and erosion has created dramatic cuts in sedimentary rock formations, exposing fossils hidden within.

The age of the rocks determines the age of the dinosaurs that were trapped there. The time of the dinosaurs lasted 160 million years. A given sedimentary rock formation is but a window onto a small portion of that long span of time.

Dinosaur hunters do not just dig anywhere for dinosaurs. They first find a sedimentary rock formation that is as old as the dinosaurs. Then they explore its surface for evidence of fossils that might already be exposed. Returning to an area that was explored before is a good way to find new specimens. Even a few months or years of exposure to the forces of wind and rain are sometimes enough to erode the surface of a rock formation to reveal more bones. Fossils that may not have been visible twenty years ago might be baking in the sun today.

There are still parts of the world that have not been fully explored for dinosaur bones. In these places, scientists looking for dinosaurs often face challenges in the field that test their mental and physical endurance. Bones are often found in dry, rugged areas where the hot sun beats down and there are no trees to provide shelter or shade. When working in remote areas such as this, scientists must use even greater patience and persistence and work harder than normal to dig up dinosaur bones. Without such heroic efforts, there would be few dinosaurs to see in museums or to study in books.

The only hard evidence scientists have that dinosaurs ever existed are their fossils in ancient sediments of the earth. From these clues, paleontologists use their knowledge of today's animals and ecosystems and their imagination to picture a world

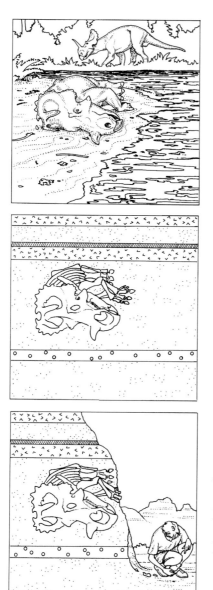

A dinosaur dies by the water's edge. Sand covers the body while the flesh rots away.

The skeleton is buried and compacted under additional layers of sediment over millions of years. Minerals from the surrounding layers absorb into the skeleton, eventually changing its composition from bone to stone. All the fine detail from the original bone material is preserved.

Erosion by wind, water, or passing glaciers exposes the fossil elements in some locations. Paleontologists explore these areas, searching for bone fragments that can lead to the discovery and excavation of long-buried dinosaur treasure.

The process of fossilization

inhabited by living dinosaurs. It is remarkable that so much can be understood about a group of animals that has not walked the earth for more than 65 million years.

In these pages you will find accounts of some of history's most exciting and important dinosaur hunting expeditions. They span the globe from the American West and the Canadian badlands to Central Asia, Africa, and South America. These journeys will take you on horseback to the American West with Buffalo Bill Cody and by riverboat through remote regions of western Canada. You will travel by camel over the sands of North Africa, by foot through the tropics of Tanzania, and by a caravan of cars, trucks, and camels into the desolate badlands of the Gobi Desert in Mongolia. These are the stories of famous expeditions that uncovered previously unknown worlds of dinosaurs, expeditions whose discoveries were entirely new to science.

Not only do these expeditions span the globe, they also span time from the earliest days of dinosaur hunting to the present day. They reveal that dinosaur hunting is alive and well all over the world. Many frontiers are yet to be explored. Maybe you will one day join an expedition and discover a never-before-known kind of dinosaur. But before you do, sit back and enjoy these tales of exploration that added significantly to our knowledge of dinosaurs.

CHAPTER 2

THE DINOSAUR BONE RUSH IN AMERICA

COMO BLUFF, WYOMING, 1877–1889

Dinosaur science as we know it today was new in the nineteenth century. Most fossil experts of the time were trained in other fields, particularly medicine, animal biology, or geology.

Two of the first and most famous paleontologists in America were Edward Drinker Cope of Philadelphia, Pennsylvania, and Othniel Charles Marsh of New Haven, Connecticut. Both men studied dinosaurs found in the American West in the 1870s and 1880s, before the Plains Indians were defeated. After several active years of exploring for fossils in person, both Cope and Marsh found even greater success by hiring crews of fossil hunters to find and dig the bones for them.

Cope and Marsh were not the first scientists to search for dinosaur bones. By 1842, in England, enough fossil evidence had been found there to inspire Richard Owen, a London scientist, to invent a new term: *Dinosauria,* or *dinosaurs* for short. But before Cope and Marsh got involved, only a handful of dinosaurs were known and very little about them was understood. By the time young Cope named his first dinosaur in 1866, you could still count the important dinosaurs known to science on your fingers. By 1897, after thirty more years of exploring, Cope and Marsh had personally added thirty-seven new dinosaurs that are still recognized today. Among these were the familiar *Apatosaurus, Stegosaurus, Camarasaurus, Triceratops,* and *Allosaurus.*

Stegosaurus

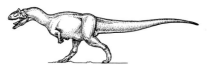

Allosaurus

Cope and Marsh were the first paleontologists who organized scientific expeditions for the purpose of finding dinosaur bones. These expeditions perfected methods that are still used today for digging and protecting fossils. Both also learned the value of popularizing the science of dinosaurs by writing and lecturing to ordinary citizens about these mysterious creatures from the past.

Cope and Marsh might have become good friends because of their love for dinosaurs. Instead, the opposite happened. Though friends as young men, they became bitter rivals, and

Edward Drinker Cope

their dislike of each other lasted their whole adult lives. They were always out for themselves, always seeking the upper hand on the other in the discovery and naming of new dinosaurs.

Until Cope and Marsh, most paleontologists stayed close to home and their museums. They studied fossils that were sent to them from all over America by curious amateurs hoping to make a little pocket money. Things changed for Marsh in 1870. His rich uncle, George Peabody, had given Yale University money to build a natural history museum. As a condition of the gift, the university was asked to put his nephew Othniel in charge of the collections. With an empty museum to fill, Marsh decided that a dramatic course of action was necessary. He decided to go west and search for fossils himself.

The First Fossil-Hunting Expeditions

The first Yale expedition left New Haven in the summer of 1870, heading for areas known to have fossil beds. They traveled by train to the army outpost nearest the desired fossil location. An army fort was the best place—often the only place—to buy food, cookware, ammunition, wagons, and mule teams.

Marsh's first expedition included twelve men, mostly Yale students. Few of them had a serious interest in fossils. According to one, they didn't have "any motive for going other than the hope of an adventure with wild game or wild Indians."[1] Marsh gave them pickaxes for digging and rifles for hunting game and protecting themselves.

The Great Plains and upper Missouri territories of the American West were the home of Native Americans. Although a generation of American settlers from the east had traveled through the area on their way to California and Oregon, few had actually settled on the plains occupied by the Indians. From the Canadian border to Texas, the great buffalo-hunting warrior societies—the Sioux, the Blackfeet, the Cheyenne, and the Comanche—had yet to be overtaken by the U.S. Army. The Sioux, under Chief Red Cloud, had just fought the army to a standstill. The last successful uprisings by Sitting Bull and Crazy Horse were still to come. Great herds of buffalo—millions of them— still populated the plains.

Othniel Charles Marsh

Marsh was headed for the lands of the Sioux and asked the U.S. Army about the possibility of providing him with military protection. To his surprise, the army not only promised an escort but invited him to find shelter at any army post in the West.

From the forts, Marsh's expeditionary team ventured into the field for days and weeks at a time, camping in the wild, digging fossils, hunting for food, and living off the land. The presence of soldiers sometimes swelled the size of the field party to as many as seventy. Marsh's first expedition even attracted the famous military guide William "Buffalo Bill" Cody. Marsh's love of the outdoors and skills as a marksman made him popular with Buffalo Bill and the army troops. They hunted buffalo together.

Most of the fossils found on the first Yale expedition were the remains of the marvelous extinct mammals that lived in the Wyoming area after the age of the dinosaurs. In Kansas, Marsh also found America's first specimen of a pterosaur—an extinct flying reptile from the time of the dinosaurs.

Marsh followed the first Yale expedition with three more in 1871, 1872, and 1873. Each traveled to the same general territory and found fossil beds brimming with additional examples of prehistoric mammals. In four short years, Marsh had created a foundation collection for the Yale Peabody Museum consisting of many tons of fossils.

Marsh's success stirred the jealously of Cope in Philadelphia. Cope soon followed Marsh into the field, exploring some of

Marsh's own cherished fossil locations and competing for the same kinds of strange and never-before-seen mammal bones.

The Dinosaur Competition Begins

In 1877, the attention of the two scientists turned to dinosaurs because of a letter from a schoolteacher near the town of Morrison, Colorado, an area just a few miles west of present-day Denver. Arthur Lakes had found some unusually large fossil bones and first wrote a letter to Marsh to find out if the scientist would be interested in buying them. Marsh was curious, but instead of jumping at the chance, he politely offered to identify the bones if Lakes would send them to Yale in Connecticut. No deal was struck.

Othniel Charles Marsh (center) led the Yale Expedition in 1870.

Before too long, Lakes discovered more bones, including what looked like a gigantic leg, and wrote to Marsh again. Lakes estimated that the total length of the animal must have been 60 to 70 feet (18 to 21 meters), a figure that must have sounded unbelievably big at the time. This time Lakes took more direct action. He packed up ten crates of the bones and shipped them to Marsh at Yale, hoping to ignite the scientist's curiosity and loosen his wallet.

As a fallback, Lakes also sent a few of the spectacular bones to Cope in Philadelphia.

Cope was the first to act. Because of his previous study of dinosaur bones, he immediately recognized the bones to be those of another dinosaur. He was delighted at his good fortune but unaware that Marsh had already been approached about the same specimen. Cope set to work writing a scientific description of the dinosaur, but the dinosaur wasn't his for long.

Finally answering the letters from Lakes, Marsh took action and quickly got the upper hand. He fired off a check to Lakes for one hundred dollars. But, he warned, he wanted the entire specimen, including the bones that had been sent to Cope. Unfortunately for Cope, he had not yet paid Lakes for any of the bones, and so had to pack them up and send them to Marsh in Connecticut.

So it was that Othniel C. Marsh identified his first new dinosaur, without having set one foot out of New Haven, Connecticut. The dinosaur was a long-necked plant eater.

Marsh acted quickly to take over the bone site that Lakes had found. He wanted to make sure that Cope did not invade his turf. He sent his most trusted field men with Lakes to set up camp in Colorado and continue digging for every dinosaur they could find there.

Arthur Lakes had some good ideas about digging fossil bones. He was an amateur painter and got in the habit of sketching the fossil bones while they were still in the ground. These sketches would prove to be valuable when the scientists tried to piece the bones back together in Marsh's preparation lab in New Haven. Lakes also improved upon a method invented by one of Cope's field men for protecting fossil bones on the long, bouncy trip back East. He soaked burlap strips in plaster of paris and then wrapped these around the outside of a chunk of fossil bone. The strips hardened to form a durable protective coating or "jacket." This jacket was much like a cast worn to protect a broken leg. Once back at the museum, the plaster strips could be chipped off to reveal the valuable fossils once again. This method of creating a fossil jacket is still used today.

The skeletons that Lakes had found were spectacular. Most were the remains of gigantic long-necked plant eaters. But the fossils were difficult to dig out, and they were also incomplete. It was easy for Marsh to confuse one kind of dinosaur with another. Even so, one fact was certain: These creatures were much larger and far different than anything found before. Marsh named the first one *Titanosaurus* ("giant lizard"). He declared that it was the largest of "any land animal hitherto discovered."[2] He thought that the complete dinosaur would measure about 50 to 60 feet (15 to 18 meters) long from its nose to the tip of its tail.

Cope's disappointment over the Lakes dinosaur did not last long. About 80 miles (130 kilometers) south of that location, near Canon City, Colorado, a school superintendent named O. W. Lucas discovered another fossil bed filled with extremely large dinosaur bones. They dated from about the same era as those from Marsh's quarry but they were in better condition and easier to dig out. Fortunately for Cope, Lucas contacted him first. Cope acted in a flash. He immediately bought the first sample bones sent to him by Lucas and hired a crew to help dig the bountiful site.

By late summer 1877, Cope had turned the tables on Marsh. He announced the discovery of *Camarasaurus*, another long-necked giant, "which exceeds in proportions any other land animal hitherto described, including the one found by Professor Arthur Lakes."[3] Both Cope and Marsh had chanced upon a lesser known period of dinosaurs. Even they were surprised by what was being found. Leg bones the size of tree trunks! Back bones as big around as wagon wheels! The more they dug, the more they were astonished. The age of the bones was determined by understanding the age of the geologic

Othniel Marsh named *Titanosaurus*, a long-necked plant eater with plates on its skin.

deposits in which they were found. Cope and Marsh were uncovering a world of the plant-eating giants dating back over 150 million years.

Marsh eventually abandoned the fossil site in Morrison to seek better specimens. Later that same summer, he received a mysterious letter from Wyoming. Signed by two gentlemen calling themselves Harlow and Edwards, the letter described a

Edward Cope announced the discovery of *Camarasaurus*, which had leg bones as big as tree trunks.

fantastic bone bed near Laramie, Wyoming. All these men wanted was some money for their trouble, which Marsh was ever so happy to provide.[4] The two men turned out to be railroad supervisors. They had at first used false names when they wrote to Marsh, hoping to guard their identity and the location of the fossils. Once a deal was struck, they revealed themselves as W. E. Carlin and W. H. Reed.

Marsh sent his best men to the newly discovered fossil site in Wyoming. The bone bed came to be called Como Bluff. The dinosaur bones were spread across 6 miles (10 kilometers) of rocky terrain. Many individual quarries were dug across this expanse. Although not as densely packed with bones as some other smaller sites, Como Bluff still ranks today as one of the most plentiful dinosaur deposits ever discovered.

Marsh's team of workers remained at Como Bluff for six and a half years, removing ton after ton of dinosaur bones. By the time they were finished, nearly five hundred crates of dinosaur bones had been shipped from Como Bluff to New Haven.

Marsh named more than two dozen new dinosaurs from these remains, including some of the most famous dinosaurs of all. Several long-necked dinosaurs were found there, such as *Brontosaurus* (now known as *Apatosaurus*, or "deceptive lizard"), *Diplodocus* ("double-beam"), and *Camarasaurus* ("chambered lizard"). Perhaps the strangest dinosaur they found was *Stegosaurus*

Diplodocus

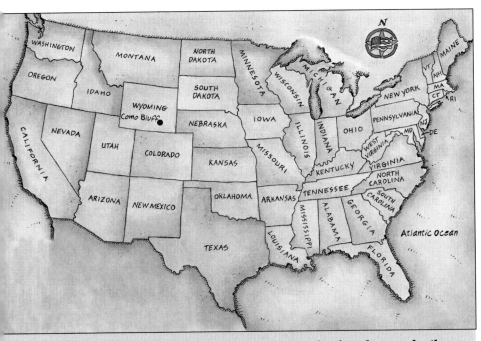

Como Bluff in Wyoming ranks as one of the most abundant dinosaur fossil sites ever discovered.

("plated lizard"), the plant eater with a double row of large triangular plates on its back and spikes on its tail. The likely target of those spikes was also found at Como Bluff. It was the largest meat-eating dinosaur known at the time, *Allosaurus* ("different lizard").

A fossil site as rich as Como Bluff was bound to attract fossil hunters who worked for Cope. Expecting this, Marsh posted armed guards around the site, ordering them to chase off any strangers. It was a big territory, though, and even Marsh's guards could not prevent Cope from sending his own team into parts of the surrounding area.

One summer day in 1879, rumors circulated among Marsh's men that Edward D. Cope himself was going to pay them a visit. Secretly, many of Marsh's men were curious to meet the man whom Marsh had portrayed as such a villain. The visit came to pass and Cope was an instant success with Marsh's men. Lakes himself found Cope to be a "very agreeable" fellow.[5]

If Cope learned anything from his visit, it was that his team in Wyoming was much less successful than Marsh's. Ironically, the most spectacular fossil Cope's men dug up—a fine specimen of a large meat eater—went neglected by Cope for a long time. By the time he took a close look at it, Marsh had already found a similar specimen and named it himself. It was *Allosaurus.*

Who Won?

The great dinosaur bone rush that began with Cope and Marsh in 1877 occupied the two men until their deaths. Cope died in 1897 and Marsh in 1899. The fierce competition between them led to many new dinosaur discoveries, but many mistakes as well. Of the 149 dinosaur species named by Cope and Marsh, only 37 are accepted by paleontologists today. Many of the species they thought were new have proved to be different individuals belonging to the same species. Some of this confusion happened because dinosaur science was so new. Remember, these two men were unearthing a parade of strange creatures that had never been seen before. They were bound to make some mistakes, and science is, after all, one continuous series of discoveries, each improving upon our previous understanding. However, many mistakes were made by Cope and Marsh because they were too eager to triumph in their fossil feud. They could have prevented many of the errors by taking more time to study the evidence and by looking for additional fossils to fill in the gaps in their knowledge. They also could have tried to work together. Instead, they often jumped to conclusions that were later proved to be wrong.[6]

Of course error, and the correction of error, are vital parts of science. Cope and Marsh opened up a vast frontier in the study of dinosaurs. In so doing, they also laid the foundation for future expeditions by other scientists who learned from the mistakes of these two feuding professors.

CHAPTER 3

A DINOSAUR SAFARI IN AFRICA

TENDAGURU, TANZANIA, 1909–1913

In the early 1900s, nobody was expecting to find a vast deposit of dinosaur bones in East Africa. The wilds of Tanzania were known for their tree-shrouded hills and open plains, where lions chased their galloping prey and swarms of tsetse flies hovered in dense clouds over tall grasses. The area contrasted sharply with the forbidding badlands of Wyoming, where dinosaurs had previously been found. In 1907, however, the name Tendaguru was thrust into the headlines and became linked with high adventure and perhaps the most ambitious dinosaur expedition ever undertaken anywhere in the world.

The giant dinosaurs discovered at Como Bluff were not alone in their world. During the Late Jurassic Period (150 million years ago), when the continents of the world had not yet grown so far apart, Marsh's famous giants were roaming

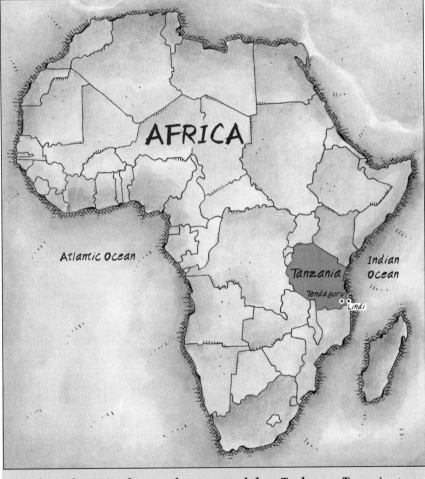

In the early 1900s, dinosaur hunters traveled to Tendaguru, Tanzania, to investigate a large find of fossil bones.

Wyoming. Curiously, some of the same dinosaurs were also found in Tanzania, a country along the eastern part of Africa. Scientists believe that until the end of the Jurassic Period, the continents were still in contact with each other, which allowed dinosaurs to wander over much of the earth. By the end of the age of dinosaurs, this was no longer possible, and there is a striking difference in the dinosaurs found in the Northern and Southern Hemispheres of the world.

The most famous Late Jurassic dinosaur beds of Africa are located in Tendaguru, about 40 miles (65 kilometers) inland from the coastal city of Lindi. It was a site where many dinosaurs died.

Discovery of Dinosaur Fossils in Tendaguru

By the early twentieth century, many parts of Africa had been colonized by European nations. Tanzania was a part of German East Africa. The dinosaur-hunting story of Tendaguru began with a visit by a German engineer working for a German mining company. While searching for minerals in the region, he noticed a sizable outcrop of fossil bones. Although the engineer was not a paleontologist, he immediately recognized the importance of the bones and informed his company.

Word of the discovery spread to Professor Eberhard Fraas of Stuttgart, Germany, who happened to be visiting Tanzania at the time. He was one of Germany's leading paleontologists and an expert on fossil reptiles. Fraas inspected the site himself and was astonished at what he saw. It appeared that there were probably tons of large dinosaur bones waiting to be excavated. His enthusiasm got the best of him. He gathered up several samples and took them back to Stuttgart for examination.

Unfortunately for him, Fraas was stricken with dysentery while on the return trip to Germany. He would be unable to return to Tendaguru to excavate the magnificent fossils. But he did the next best thing: He told his colleagues back in Germany about the find and sought funds to send an expedition to retrieve the bounty. His efforts paid off. The director of the Berlin Museum, Wilhelm von Branca, became interested in Tendaguru and helped form an elite committee to raise the funds needed for the expedition. Support flowed in from museums, universities, the city of Berlin, and the German government. Very soon, Branca had collected a small fortune to support a sizable fossil-hunting team in Tendaguru for four successive field trips. This exceeded Branca's wildest expectations.

Branca knew that digging dinosaurs in the wilds of Africa would be a costly and difficult task. The team faced many serious obstacles. The climate was tropical and drenched by rains. The digging itself was not so much in rock but in soil among a thicket of trees and stubborn roots. There were no roads or trails to the site, requiring about 40 miles (65 kilometers) of travel over rough terrain. There were also no motor vehicles. It took four days to walk from the coastal city of Lindi to the fossil beds in Tendaguru. All of their supplies and equipment—and tons of bones that were dug up—had to be transported on the heads and backs of the many native porters who regularly walked between the site and Lindi. The same methods had to be used to transport food and water for the many Tanzanians who worked the site. It was a challenge unlike any previous fossil expedition, and unlike any since.

The German explorers visited Tendaguru for four years to dig dinosaurs. For the first three years, from 1909 through 1911, the mission was run by German paleontologist Werner Janensch from the Berlin Museum. Janensch was himself an able field explorer, but nobody had ever attempted to dig for fossils on such a grand scale in a tropical environment before. His German assistant was Edwin Hennig. The task of actually supervising many of the workers at the dig site, however, fell to a local named Boheti bin Amrani. Amrani was a quick

The leader of the German Tendaguru expedition, Werner Janensch, and one of his African assistants.

learner and mastered the art of finding and digging dinosaur bones quickly. He was an invaluable member of the team. Not only did he discover some of the bones that were eventually dug up and shipped to Germany, but he oversaw the huge task of directing the hundreds of African workers. Work continued in 1912, but under the supervision of another German, Hans Reck, who was able to give Janensch and Hennig a well-deserved break from the field so that they could return to Berlin to study the tons of fossils that had already been found.

An African field crew carries crates filled with dinosaur fossils discovered at Tendaguru. They traveled about forty miles to the port of Lindi.

A Small Village of Workers

The Germans were wise in how they spent their money. Most of it went to support the large number of laborers that were needed to carry the packs of supplies over the four-day hike to the site, dig the fossils, and haul them back. In the first year, they recruited 170 native workers. The work increased in the second year, requiring 400 workers. The third and fourth seasons required as many as 500 laborers each—fossil digging on a scale that has never been equaled. But that was not all. Many of the workers brought their families with them. This turned the fossil site into a small village with as many as 900 mouths to feed. Since drinkable water could not be found nearby, and food was scarce, the porters were continually traveling between Tendaguru and Lindi.

Digging up fossils in the hard-packed earth of Tendaguru was much different than working in the rocky badlands of the western United States. Hills containing fossils first had to be cleared of trees and thorny bushes that covered the surfaces. The largest hill—dubbed Tendaguru Hill—was at the center of the operation. It was at the foot of this hill that the scientists and workers set up their temporary camp. The work could not have been completed without the many hands available to clear the vegetation and dig the huge pits that revealed the mountain of bones lying beneath. This was all done using the most common tools imaginable: shovels and picks.

As the work continued, numerous fossil-bearing pits spread out from Tendaguru Hill until the entire work area covered nearly 2 square miles (5 square kilometers). The walls of the pits were often steep and stretched for 30 feet (9 meters) or more. Once a pit had been exposed to the elements, the fossils, and workers, were in danger of being harmed by rock slides or even mud slides caused by heavy rains. To prevent the sides of the huge pits from crumbling, protective coverings were thatched from tree branches and laid on the steepest sides of the pits.

Workers excavated huge pits at Tendaguru. The walls were reinforced with vegetation to prevent them from caving in.

Most of the dinosaur fossils were of large animals, making their collection somewhat burdensome, but not overly vulnerable to the brute force used to dig them up and haul them out. Workers were trained to cover the individual bones with a protective jacket of burlap and plaster, much as Marsh had done at Como Bluff in Wyoming. The bones were then hauled back to Lindi by porters and transported by ship to Germany for study.

What was it that caused so many dinosaur bones to be deposited in such a concentrated area? The bones were often jumbled and mixed together, suggesting that the remains of the dead dinosaurs had been channeled by strong waters into a bend or lagoon, where they were eventually covered by sediment and then fossilized. The bones of the dinosaurs are found in alternating layers with mud and seashells, suggesting that the area had once been a place where a freshwater river met a saltwater ocean. When the dinosaurs were present, the ocean was probably kept at bay by a natural land dam or sand bar. But sometimes the level of the ocean apparently rose up for long periods and blanketed the dinosaur graveyard with the remains of sea life.

During the four years that the German team worked the site at Tendaguru, an astounding number of fossils were dug up, packed, and sent to Germany. The individual fossil bones numbered in the thousands. When packed in their protective plaster jackets, their total weight was about 250 tons (225 metric tons). These were packed in crates and individually carried by porters during 5,400 trips from the Tendaguru fossil village to Lindi.[1]

Once back in Germany, the fossils presented another daunting challenge: that of cleaning, identifying, and assembling the material so that the scientists could determine what kinds of animals they had found. The laboratory preparation of the Tendaguru fossils took many years. Werner Janensch and Edwin Hennig were among the team of paleontologists that studied the bones at the Berlin Museum. Some of the bones were broken into many pieces on the journey to Germany and required many long hours of restoration. A six-foot- (two-meter-) long shoulder blade from one of the sauropods, or long-necked plant eaters, required 160 hours of lab work before the pieces could be adequately and securely put back together. An even more extreme example was a giant single back bone that took 450 hours to clean and piece back together. The Tendaguru fossil collection kept a small army of fossil technicians busy for many years.[2]

Dinosaur Giants of Tendaguru

The results were spectacular. Several dinosaurs that were first discovered by Marsh and others in North America also showed up in Tendaguru. Among these were *Barosaurus* ("heavy lizard," Marsh 1890), *Dryosaurus* ("tree lizard," Marsh 1894), and the giant *Brachiosaurus* ("arm lizard," Riggs 1903). *Brachiosaurus* is one of the largest known dinosaurs. This long-necked giant stood about 40 feet (12 meters) tall with its towering long neck and heavy body. Only *Argentinosaurus* and

Paralititan are considered larger and heavier. The fossil specimen of *Brachiosaurus* mounted in the Berlin Museum is the largest dinosaur skeleton found in any museum that is made of real fossil bone.

In addition, several new dinosaurs were discovered at Tendaguru. They include

- *Dicraeosaurus* ("forked lizard"), another long-necked plant eater, but less stupendous at 40 feet (12 meters) long.

- *Kentrosaurus* ("spiked lizard"), a spiky-tailed stegosaur with small triangular plates on its back.

- *Elaphrosaurus* ("fleet lizard"), a light, slender meat eater.

- *Tornieria* (named for German paleontologist Gustav Tornier), a lightly built long-necked plant eater.

Kentrosaurus was one of the dinosaurs discovered in Tendaguru. This spiky-tailed stegosaur could probably rear up on its hind legs to reach high plants.

The German team from the Berlin Museum concluded its visits to Tendaguru in 1912. Although word had spread around the world about their spectacular discoveries, few expeditions have returned to seek additional bones because of the difficulty of working there. One series of British expeditions from 1924 to 1929 met with some success. This was largely because they went back to the same spot that had attracted the Germans years earlier. They also hired Boheti bin Amrani, the able overseer of the German crews, to supervise their digs. Without his help, their efforts would have been much less successful. As one member of the British team admitted, "Without Boheti, the element of chance involved in the question, Where shall we dig next? would have assumed almost overwhelming proportions. At first, at any rate, as far as we could see, bones might be anywhere, only they weren't."[3]

The German expedition to Africa put the giant continent on the map of dinosaur finds. It inspired many subsequent expeditions to explore various parts of the continent, most notably South Africa, the deserts of North Africa and Egypt, and nearby Madagascar off the East African coast. But they all began with the unbelievable success and mind-boggling challenges of the German expeditions to Tendaguru.

CHAPTER 4

THE LOST AND FOUND DINOSAURS OF EGYPT

EXPEDITIONS OF 1910–1914 AND 2000

The history of Egypt includes more than mummies and pyramids. Some of the world's largest and most unusual dinosaurs once roamed the same territory many millions of years before the ancient Egyptians. These dinosaur bones are now buried in the sand-encrusted rocks that can be found in certain parts of the Sahara desert.

What is now a stark and unforgiving desert was once a lush mangrove swamp in the time of the dinosaurs. The area was near the Tethys Sea, a shallow prehistoric ocean that once covered much of Europe and North Africa, separating them from India and Asia. The land resembled the mangrove islands of the Florida Everglades today. It was teeming with life of all

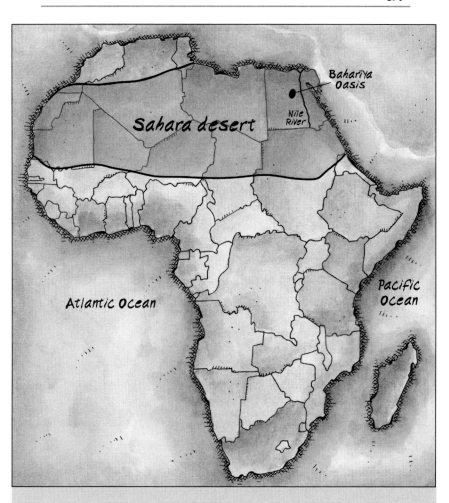

The Sahara desert in Africa was once a lush swamp where dinosaurs lived.

kinds—tropical plants, fish, amphibians, reptiles, oceangoing reptiles, and dinosaurs.

Africa was a popular place for German-sponsored dinosaur expeditions in the early part of the twentieth century. At about the same time as the German dinosaur safari in

Tendaguru, another German explorer took an interest in the fossils of Egypt.

Egypt, in North Africa, is mainly known for the remains of ancient civilizations. Explorers in the land of the pyramids were mostly interested in discovering the hidden treasures of the pharaohs. Under their noses were some of the most spectacular dinosaur fossils yet to be discovered.

Earlier fossil hunters from Germany, Great Britain, and America had explored Egypt. One expedition from the American Museum of Natural History was led by Walter Granger in 1907. They found a wealth of mammal fossils dating from about 35 to 45 million years ago. These fossils were younger than those of dinosaurs by 20 to 30 million years, but tempting to dinosaur hunters nonetheless. Were there dinosaurs to be found in the land of the pharaohs?

Richard Markgraf was an important Austrian fossil hunter living in Cairo, Egypt. He suffered from poor health and moved to Egypt to tend to a respiratory problem. The former violinist liked Egypt and learned the language quickly. This knowledge and his talent for finding fossils made him a popular worker for European and American museums. When Walter Granger of the American Museum of Natural History met him in 1907, he described Markgraf this way: "We find him very agreeable. . . . Herr M. lives in a tiny tent with bare necessities; has two camels and two men. Speaks Arabic well."[1]

Richard Markgraf was an Austrian fossil hunter living in Cairo, Egypt.

Stromer Stumbles Upon Dinosaurs

The presence of mammal fossils in the Egyptian desert was known to young German paleontologist Baron Ernst Stromer von Reichenbach of the University of Munich. In late 1910 he ventured into the desert about 160 miles (260 kilometers) southwest of Cairo accompanied only by a guide, a cook, four camels, and two camel drivers. He was hoping to find more spectacular mammal fossils like the ones that Walter Granger had discovered. Instead, he and his party wound up about 100 miles from the Granger site and stumbled across something completely unexpected: dinosaurs! The rocks were about

This is the Baharīya Oasis as it looks today, about 160 miles from the city of Cairo.

60 million years older than he had expected. They dated from a time when giant predatory dinosaurs ruled a much greener and wetter Egypt. This surprise proved to be both a blessing and a curse for the young scientist. These dinosaurs would control the young man's destiny.

Stromer immediately set to work on the rich fossil site. The area is known as the Baharīya Oasis. He faced many of the same physical and climatic challenges that Granger's team had encountered. Stromer wisely hired the experienced Richard Markgraf to help him.

The forbidding working conditions in the western desert of Egypt were nothing like the wet and balmy savanna of Tendaguru. Field work was best carried out in the early months of the year—before June, when the devastating heat set in. The days were still hot but the nights were cold and required overcoats. Sandstorms were possible in the day or night. Even when there weren't any sandstorms, the wind could whip violently, sending a fine sandy dust through the air and into the eyes of the workers. The team also confronted an extremely itchy problem—the area was often infested with annoying fleas, probably riding on the hides of the camels.

Richard Markgraf was an invaluable and experienced member of Stromer's expedition. He was accustomed to living out of a tent and traveling the desert on camel. His language skills enabled the Germans to effectively train and supervise the Egyptian workers that they employed.

Markgraf was also an inventive fossil collector. He devised a method of making glue from local vegetation to help preserve the fossils. Walter Granger described it this way: "Markgraf uses hot glue for hardening bones. Has the Arab collect dead brush and boil the glue and applies while hot and thin. Seems to penetrate and harden well."[2]

A similar technique—using glue from a bottle—is still used today to harden fragmentary fossils before they are dug completely out of the ground. This joins the fragments so that the bone won't crumble when it is removed.

The fine sandstone in which the fossils were encased consisted of crusty sand and small pebbles. It had to be removed to see whether any fossils lay beneath the surface. If it were removed too vigorously, as with a pick or shovel, the delicate fossils encased within would be easily damaged. The fossils were so fragmented that they would easily fall apart into hundreds of shards if not dug up carefully.

Markgraf perfected a clever method of removing this top layer of sandstone to reveal what was hidden beneath. He broke and brushed away a small part of the crusty surface and then let the wind take over. Given the strong gusts, a small opening in the surface would gently become bigger and bigger, revealing whether a fossil lay beneath. Many such test cuts could be made at the same time while the crew worked on other parts of the dig. If a fossil was revealed by one of these surface excavations, the workers would take over and carefully chip away the surrounding sandstone using brushes and small tools. The trick was to remove layers of sandstone to expose fragile fossil bone, then apply glue to keep the bone together before it was removed for packing.[3]

A Sail-Back Dinosaur and More

Stromer and Markgraf made a great team. Before too long, the Egyptian desert was revealing a remarkable world of prehistoric life-forms. The fossils did not include only dinosaurs. There were also the remains of an entire coastal ecosystem from about 100 million years ago.

In three years of digging, the team discovered as many as fifty new kinds of animals and plants, including fish, turtles, marine reptiles, and crocodiles. Most impressive were four new kinds of dinosaurs. Three of them were surprisingly large meat eaters, and one was a sizable long-necked, plant-eating sauropod.

Ernst Stromer discovered the meat-eating dinosaur *Spinosaurus* in the Egyptian desert.

The most spectacular of Stromer's meat eaters was *Spinosaurus* ("spiny lizard"), the big bad monster that was the star of the movie *Jurassic Park III*. It rivaled *Tyrannosaurus* ("tyrant lizard") in length but was more lightly built than its North American cousin. Most unusual about *Spinosaurus* was a sail on its back that was at some points 6 feet (1.8 meters) tall. The head and jaw of *Spinosaurus* were also more crocodile-like, leading scientists to think that it may have been a fish eater.

The two other meat eaters dug up by the team were less complete than *Spinosaurus*. *Bahariasaurus* ("Baharīya lizard," after the Baharīya Oasis fossil location) is known mainly from an upper leg bone that is equal to the size of that found in a moderately large *Tyrannosaurus*. More interesting is

Carcharodontosaurus ("shark-toothed lizard"), of which only skull fragments, some neck and shoulder bones, teeth, and other scattered remains were found. It was clearly a big beast. Just *how* big wasn't dreamed until 1995 when a new discovery was made in North Africa. An American expedition to Morocco led by paleontologist Paul Sereno dug up a new skull of *Carcharodontosaurus*. This individual was larger than Stromer's and had a skull measuring almost 6 feet (1.8 meters) long. With a skull this large, the length of *Carcharodontosaurus* was estimated to be 45 feet (13.7 meters). That would be 5 feet (1.5 meters) longer than *Tyrannosaurus!*

The long-necked plant eater discovered by Stromer was named *Aegyptosaurus* ("Egypt lizard"). It is known mostly from limb bones that showed that it was a medium-sized sauropod measuring between 50 and 60 feet (15 and 18 meters) long.

By the time that Stromer returned to Germany, he had so many fossils that it took him the next twenty years to unpack and study them.

Stromer's Bad Luck

The story of Stromer's magnificent dinosaurs has many unfortunate twists. After his expeditions were finished in 1914, he had great difficulty shipping the fossils to Germany, where he wanted to study them. This was the time of World War I, when Great Britain and Germany were facing off on the battlefields of Europe. Cairo was controlled by the British, and this delayed Stromer's ability to ship the fossils to Germany for many years. His troubles were by no means over once he was able to ship the fossils. Many of the valuable specimens were broken in transit. It wasn't until the 1920s and 1930s that he was able to thoroughly study the magnificent Baharīya fossils and write about them for science.

As if these setbacks were not enough, one final blow was to propel Stromer into relative obscurity for many years. In 1944, Great Britain and Germany were once again at war. Stromer was safe in his Munich museum, but the curse of the Egyptian fossils was about to come to a disastrous conclusion. The fossils that represented his life's work—including his four important dinosaurs—were stored in the Munich museum where Stromer worked. On April 24, 1944, the British Royal Air Force bombed a military target in Munich. All the fossils were destroyed when the air raid accidentally set fire to the museum.[4] All that remained of the spectacular fossils were Stromer's stories, field notes, and published descriptions, drawings, and photographs.

A Return to Egypt

Stromer's lost dinosaurs have haunted paleontologists ever since. Even the precise location of his Baharīya site had been forgotten. Then, in 1999 and 2000, a new team of dinosaur hunters from the University of Pennsylvania and the Egyptian Geological Museum decided to try to locate Stromer's treasure site and begin to dig again.

In 1999, armed only with Stromer's sketchy field notes, Josh Smith and Jennifer Smith, two graduate students from the University of Pennsylvania, visited Egypt in search of the famed fossil site. Josh Smith was studying paleontology with dinosaur expert Peter Dodson, and Jennifer was working on a degree in geology. Having only three days in the field to search for the site, and equipped only with Stromer's handwritten notes and drawings, the pair drove out into the desert looking for clues. Josh recalls that they really got lucky. "I'm hanging my head out of the car window at thirty miles an hour and I see a bone," remembers Josh.[5] More bones lay in the vicinity. This became the first of about twenty accumulations of bones that they found in the area. They also spotted a land formation that resembled one described by Stromer. This seemed to be the correct location of Stromer's lost fossil site. Not having any time to actually dig the site, they noted the location and headed back to tell Dodson and their other colleagues about the exciting find.

Jen, Josh, and a team including Peter Dodson from the University of Pennsylvania returned in force in 2000 and began a hopeful dig. Arriving in the early months of the year, the team hoped to avoid the sweltering heat of the sun. The temperatures swung wildly from nighttime lows of near freezing to daytime highs of 90 degrees Fahrenheit (32 degrees Celsius). Unlike Stromer, however, they did not have to live in tents in the desert. Instead, they took up residence in a pleasant motel that served as their home for the duration of the dig.

Returning to one of the bone sites that Jen and Josh had noted the year before, the team dug in and soon uncovered several more impressive parts of a very large skeleton. By the time they were finished, they had recovered about a quarter of the skeleton of an extremely large long-necked plant-eating dinosaur. It turned out to be the second-largest known sauropod, which they named *Paralititan*, or "tidal giant," after the coastal tidal environment in which the dinosaur once lived. It was a stocky beast about 80 to 100 feet (24 to 30 meters) long and weighing as much as 70 tons (63.5 metric tons). Only *Argentinosaurus*, a relative found in South America, was bigger and bulkier. Along with Stromer's original finds, *Paralititan* adds significantly to the legacy of Egyptian dinosaurs.

The team also rediscovered some of the excavation pits that Stromer's team had made eighty-eight years before. But nothing much was to be found in them. Stromer's team had

Team members Allison Tumarkin and Matt Lamanna stretch out next to the upper arm bone (humerus) of *Paralititan* in Egypt.

Paralititan was a very large, long-necked, plant-eating dinosaur.

done a thorough job. University of Pennsylvania team member Matt Lamanna, however, stumbled across something even more important and exciting. While hiking alone back to camp one day, he found himself walking among tons of fossil bones littering the ground all around him. The fossils not only included dinosaurs but fish bones, turtle shells, plants, and other important material. It was the remains of an environment in which many kinds of animals had died. This kind of evidence is valuable for scientists because it helps paint a picture of the complete environment in which the dinosaurs lived. The team also found abundant evidence, mostly in the form of small teeth, that some smaller kinds of meat-eating dinosaurs were walking around with the plant-eating giants.

While nobody has yet to discover another spectacular specimen of Stromer's *Spinosaurus*, Paul Sereno has had great success in discovering several other new dinosaurs from North Africa. See Chapter 7 for the story of dinosaurs of the African sands.

CHAPTER 5

THE CANADIAN DINOSAUR BONE RUSH

RED DEER RIVER, ALBERTA, 1910–1917

Dinosaur bone rushes were much like the California gold rush. Once the word was out that dinosaurs could be found in a certain place, anybody who had any business hunting dinosaurs was on his way there.

The wild badlands of Alberta, Canada, were the scene of the second great dinosaur bone rush. Like Cope and Marsh in the 1870s, two rival teams squared off to find a great assortment of new dinosaurs. Unlike Cope and Marsh, this was a friendly rivalry conducted by two well-known institutions, the American Museum of Natural History in New York City, and the Geological Survey of Canada.

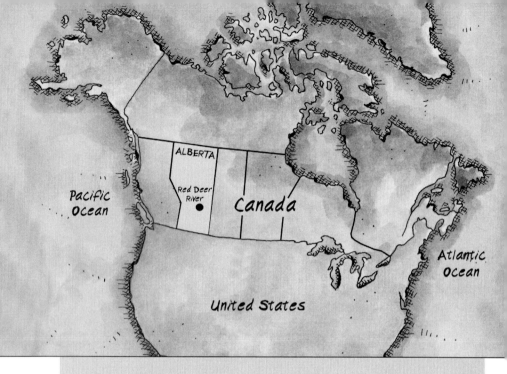

Alberta, Canada, was the scene of the second great dinosaur bone rush.

The First Hint of Dinosaurs in Alberta

The presence of abundant dinosaur bones in the badlands of Alberta became known in the 1880s. In 1884 Joseph Burr Tyrrell took a job with the Geological Survey of Canada. The Geological Survey was exploring the Alberta territory for minerals and making maps. In his travels with the Survey, Tyrrell found himself in the starkly beautiful valley of the Red Deer River in central Alberta. The fossil deposits of the region date from about 75 million years ago, a period that was later than the Wyoming finds of Como Bluff and very nearly at the end of the age of dinosaurs. Among the fossils that Tyrrell and his party found was the partial skull of an unknown predatory dinosaur. It was hauled by wagon to Calgary, Canada, and eventually shipped to Edward Cope in Philadelphia for examination. Cope declared that the Canadians had found a carnivorous dinosaur. Today, it is known as *Albertosaurus* ("Alberta lizard"), a smaller cousin of *Tyrannosaurus*.

Thirteen years later, in 1897, another Canadian named Lawrence Lambe became curious about the fossils of the Red Deer River. Lambe also worked for the Geological Survey of Canada. He was hired as an artist to illustrate fossils that were found by the Survey. While visiting Alberta, he hired a boat to take him down the Red Deer River to see what he could find.

The banks of the Red Deer River consist of steep cliffs with highly eroded slopes jutting up from the riverbank. They

Albertosaurus, a small cousin of *Tyrannosaurus*, was discovered by Joseph Burr Tyrrell and his team. Here, a group of *Albertosaurus* attacks the plant-eating dinosaur *Hypacrosaurus*.

are not easily accessed by land. It is within these cliffs and surrounding flatlands that dinosaur fossils can be found.

Lambe spotted many deposits of fossils during his river trip and returned the following year with a team to start digging. Although he recovered only a few fragmentary dinosaur bones, he went to work analyzing them back at the lab of the Geological Survey. He called upon his friend Henry Fairfield Osborn of the American Museum of Natural History to help compare the new fossils with those in the collection of the New York museum. Lambe published the results of their work in 1902. Much interest was generated by his finds, inspiring two rival teams of dinosaur hunters to set their sites on the Red Deer River. The great dinosaur bone rush of Canada was under way.

Barnum Brown– Dinosaur Hunter Extraordinaire

The first contender in the Canadian dinosaur hunt was Barnum Brown, an associate of Osborn's at the American Museum of Natural History. Brown was already a well-known fossil hunter by the time he left for Canada in 1910. Having dug dinosaurs mostly in the United States, he found the first two *Tyrannosaurus* skeletons in eastern Montana in 1902 and 1908. He had a knack for finding dinosaurs, and it is said that he probably recovered more specimens of dinosaurs than any other

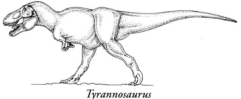

Tyrannosaurus

Barnum Brown, a paleontologist from the American Museum of Natural History, was a well-dressed gentleman with a great skill for finding dinosaur fossils.

individual. He was a well-dressed gentleman who often wore a fur coat during the chillier days of digging dinosaurs and a top hat at public events. After having found so much success digging in Montana, it was time for him to move on. Inspired by the findings of Lambe and other eyewitness accounts, he worked out a plan to dig for dinosaurs in Alberta for Osborn and the American Museum of Natural History.

Brown was not just lucky when it came to finding dinosaurs—he was inspired. He approached field work with the creativity of an artist, always seeking innovative and time-saving methods for reducing the drudgery of digging. He also thought on a grand scale—he expected big results. What else would you expect of the man who found two *T. rex?*

Brown borrowed an idea from Lambe, who had first explored the Red Deer River by boat. This seemed to be the most efficient way to access the scores of fossil deposits that awaited him there. But instead of a boat, Brown constructed a 30-foot- (9-meter-) long barge that would float lazily downstream as they searched for fossils. The barge was big enough to set up a tent on it and use as a mobile camp. Any fossils that were recovered could be easily loaded on board and transported to a spot along the river where they could be hauled up onto land, carted by wagon to a train station, and put on a train to New York City.

The expedition party began its journey down the Red Deer River on August 3, 1910. The crew was small and consisted only of Brown and two other men, one a cook. The first 60 miles (97 kilometers) of the river were treacherous, so Brown hired an experienced river man to guide them through the rapids while they all hung on for dear life. After that, they were able to float peacefully down the river, spying for fossils. They stopped frequently to inspect the riverbanks and surrounding areas and dug up whatever they found. Brown described the tranquil days as follows:

> In the long midsummer days . . . there are many hours of daylight, and constant floating would have carried us many miles per day; but frequent stops were made to prospect for fossils, and we rarely covered more than twenty miles per day. High up on the plateau buildings and haystacks proclaim a well-settled country, but habitations are rare along the river, and for miles we floated through picturesque solitude, the silence unbroken save by the noise of the rapids.[1]

It wasn't long before Brown's party was extremely busy collecting and packing up dinosaur bones. During the first season alone they crated up twenty-six boxes of bones for Osborn's museum. These specimens included dinosaurs of many varieties, including new horned dinosaurs (ceratopsians), *Trachodon* ("rough tooth," now thought to be another hadrosaur, maybe *Edmontosaurus*), the "ostrich dinosaur" *Ornithomimus* ("bird mimic"), and remnants of Canada's most common tyrannosaur, *Albertosaurus*. Brown wrote about the good fortune in the most matter-of-fact way in his field journal:

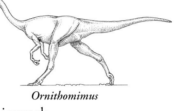

Ornithomimus

> A *Trachodon* humerus [and] poorly preserved bones were found at nearly every stop made from there on down but nothing of value until we reached the mouth of Big Valley where on the opposite west side of the river numerous bones were found especially a large quarry. Bones were most numerous in two sandstone layers about 20 and 30 ft above the river at this point. A single fragmentary skeleton was found in the first coal seam about 160 feet above the river which up to that time was the only Ceratopsian remains observed.[2]

Brown's successful river-riding formula for finding and transporting fossils worked so well that the digs continued each summer until 1916. Osborn himself visited in 1912 and rode down the river for several days with Brown. The tally of bone crates mounted up year by year, reaching a peak in 1914 when the team sent eighty-three boxes of fossils back to New

Barnum Brown sits next to a magnificent specimen of the duck-billed dinosaur *Corythosaurus*.

York. Duck-billed dinosaurs were abundant and included not only *Trachodon*, but three new kinds, *Corythosaurus* ("helmet lizard"), *Kritosaurus* ("separated lizard"), and *Saurolophus* ("crested lizard"). Meat-eating dinosaurs were represented by *Albertosaurus* and *Ornithomimus*. Horned dinosaurs were found in great numbers and included a fine specimen of *Monoclonius* ("one-horned"), a partial skeleton of *Styracosaurus* ("spiked lizard"), *Leptoceratops* ("slender-horned face"), and *Anchiceratops* ("close-horned face"). Brown also recovered a few new specimens of the armored dinosaur *Ankylosaurus*, which he had first found in Montana and named in

Styracosaurus

1908. Perhaps his biggest surprise was the recovery of a duck-billed dinosaur along with a wide patch of skin impressions—the fossilized patterns of dinosaur skin.

Enter the Sternbergs

The thought of all of these fossil treasures being shipped off to New York City eventually raised an eyebrow in Canada. It seemed unfair that so many fine specimens of Canadian dinosaurs would be on display in New York, some 2,300 miles (3,700 kilometers) away. In 1912, the government-operated Geological Survey of Canada decided to hire its own fossil-hunting team to explore the Red Deer River area. Their choice? A family of American fossil hunters from Kansas named the Sternbergs.

Charles H. Sternberg, sixty-two years old in 1912, was the head of a well-known clan of fossil hunters. Sternberg had worked with none other than Edward Drinker Cope and Othniel Charles Marsh on separate occasions. Some of the family had even been working for Barnum Brown in the United States prior to the start of the Canadian bone rush. Many of the fossils they had found were on display in world-leading museums, including the American Museum of Natural History in New York. As a family of collectors, Charles and his three sons—Charlie, Levi, and George—could certainly match Barnum Brown in their ability to find and excavate high-quality dinosaur fossils.

The Sternbergs' boss at the Geological Survey was Lawrence Lambe, the paleontologist who had started the

Canadian bone rush with his discoveries between 1897 and 1902. Lambe was admittedly not the best of field workers; he preferred to study specimens back at his office. He was more than happy to have the great Sternberg family out in the dinosaur beds, packing up and sending him specimens to describe.

The Sternbergs first went into the Red Deer River area in 1912, using a wagon team and a rowboat. Interestingly, George Sternberg had already agreed to work for Barnum Brown that summer, so he could not join his family on the rival team. As it turned out, the Sternbergs did not make it too

George Sternberg uncovers a dinosaur in Alberta, Canada.

close to the river that summer. Instead, they were occupied with digging up a fine skeleton of a duck-billed dinosaur near Drumheller, about 100 miles (160 kilometers) from where Brown was digging. The duck-billed specimen was about 32 feet (9.6 meters) long and nearly complete, but in a fractured section of rock that made its excavation extremely difficult. Before removing the fragmented bones, they had to coat them with shellac, which held them together like glue. They next sectioned the massive skeleton into parts that could be dug up separately. The bones and rock were covered with a protective layer of burlap soaked in plaster. Some of the sections weighed as much as 3,000 pounds (1,360 kilograms). It took them six weeks to remove the skeleton. Hauling it by wagon was not easy.

For the next field season, in 1913, the Sternbergs changed their tactics. George rejoined them, and they decided to take a page out of Barnum Brown's book and construct a barge on which to travel down the river. Their raft measured 12 feet square (13 square meters). It was big enough to house two tents set up back to back. They improved upon Brown's setup by using a five-horsepower motorboat to tow the barge. This allowed them to go up- or downstream with ease.

The Sternbergs' river adventures were not without incident. At one point during the 1913 season, one of the crew nearly had his head taken off by a length of barbed wire strung across the river at about head height. It caught his hat as he ducked and sent it into the river.

Both the Brown and Sternberg teams converged on the same general locality that summer. It was an area rich with fossils. There were more than enough for both groups to dig and still leave many behind to be discovered later. Their land-based camps were not very far apart, and a healthy camaraderie grew between the two teams. It was common for them to spend Sundays together, resting and picnicking.

While the conditions in the Red Deer River vicinity were typically hot, the area sometimes experienced long periods of rain and flooding. The most persistent annoyance, however, was mosquitoes. Brown showed the Sternbergs how to make nets to protect their heads from the pesky insects.

While the Sternbergs were on their raft in the Red Deer River area, they wore protective mosquito nets.

The results of the Sternberg 1913 field season were equal to those of Brown's. Charles Sternberg reported:

> We began almost at once to find a rich fauna and collected hundreds of loose bones and teeth in the bone-beds that extended for miles at two horizons through the badlands. . . . The specimens we secured of greater value, skeletons and parts of skeletons, that we collected and packed in 53 large boxes, are the following . . .[3]

The impressive list included no fewer than thirty significant dinosaur skeletons, including a splendid *Albertosaurus,* several *Trachodon,* and *Ornithomimus.* The bounty of dinosaurs continued for the remaining seasons of the Sternberg trips to the Red Deer River. Back at his office, Lawrence Lambe was continually kept busy examining and naming the many specimens that his team had found.

In addition to those already mentioned, other dinosaurs described by Lambe from the area included the horned dinosaurs *Chasmosaurus* ("wide opening lizard"), *Eoceratops* ("dawn horned face"), and *Styracosaurus;* the huge

Chasmosaurus

duck-billed dinosaur *Edmontosaurus* ("Edmonton lizard"), and a smaller one, *Gryposaurus* ("hook-nosed lizard"); specimens of the armored dinosaurs *Euoplocephalus* ("well-armored head") and *Panoplosaurus* ("fully armored lizard"); and the meat eater *Gorgosaurus* ("terrible lizard"). Like Brown, the

Euoplocephalus

Sternbergs also recovered a partial duck-billed dinosaur with skin impressions. Lambe himself has had a duck-billed dinosaur named for him—*Lambeosaurus*.

End of the Canadian Bone Rush

The end of the 1915 field season was the last for Barnum Brown in the Red Deer River, although another American Museum team continued to work the area in 1916. The Sternbergs stayed on through 1917, but without their father, who had left after 1916 because of a dispute with the Geological Survey of Canada. Although the flurry of dinosaur

The Sternbergs used this rig to lift heavy dinosaur fossils onto wagons.

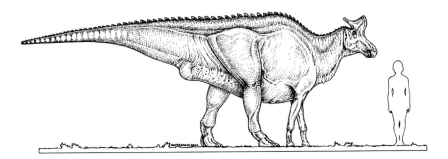

Lambeosaurus, a duck-billed, plant-eating dinosaur, was named for Lawrence Lambe. This Lambeosaurus is shown next to an adult for size comparison.

digging that characterized the bone rush was tapering off by 1918, the Sternberg brothers continued to work the Red Deer area for many more years. The most important dinosaur deposits there are now part of Dinosaur Provincial Park, where paleontologists from the Royal Tyrrell Museum of Palaeontology in Drumheller—named after Joseph Burr Tyrrell, who first discovered dinosaurs along the Red Deer River—continue to discover dinosaurs to this day. Many of the fossils discovered during the Canadian bone rush can now be seen in the American Museum of Natural History in New York City, the Royal Tyrrell Museum of Palaeontology, the Royal Ontario Museum in Toronto, and the Canadian Museum of Nature in Ottawa, Ontario.

CHAPTER 6

THE DISCOVERY OF DINOSAUR EGGS

GOBI DESERT, CENTRAL ASIA, 1922–1925

Sometimes an expedition finds something other than what it is seeking. Such was the case with the Central Asiatic Expeditions sponsored by the American Museum of Natural History in 1922, 1923, and 1925. They went to inner Mongolia—a province of China—in search of the fossil remnants of humans; they came away with dinosaurs. They also found an inhospitable climate characterized by violent sandstorms, a country in the midst of civil war, and roving bandits from which they had to protect themselves.

The search for fossil remains of early humans has fascinated paleontologists as much as finding dinosaurs. By 1900, following so much success in North America and Europe in finding the fossils of dinosaurs and mammals, paleontologists

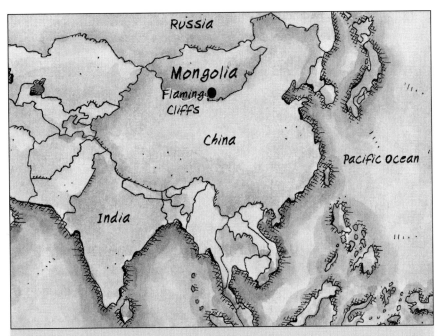

Fossil expeditions in Mongolia during the 1920s explored remote regions of Asia for fossils.

began to wonder where to find the earliest remnants of human beings. Scientists now believe that many kinds of human ancestors evolved in Africa. But around 1900, the cradle of human evolution had yet to be found.

Dreaming of Fossils in the Gobi Desert

Leading paleontologists such as Henry Fairfield Osborn of the American Museum of Natural History in New York wondered where the fossils of ancient humans could be found. By 1900, vast ranges of the world had yet to be explored. One such territory was the Gobi Desert in Central Asia. Osborn planted the seed of an idea: Perhaps ancient mammals, including man, had originated in the mysterious lands of Central Asia known as Mongolia. Mongolia is a sparsely populated land containing the Gobi Desert and its stunning rock formations.

Although the potential for finding fossils in the Gobi Desert was still unknown, Osborn's idea lit a fire under another member of the museum staff who dreamed of organizing an expedition to the Gobi. His name was Roy Chapman Andrews.

Andrews was a dashing outdoorsman and marksman. After a career of stuffing animals as a taxidermist, he went to the American Museum of Natural History to pursue his life-long dream of working in natural science. His first job at the museum was scrubbing floors, but he soon graduated to making a life-sized papier-mâché model of a whale. This was followed by expeditions in North America to collect whale bones. At the same time, he finished studies at Columbia University in New York, where he studied zoology. He was often seen in the field wearing a broad-brimmed hat and packing a loaded pistol. This image of Andrews is said to have been the original inspiration for the fictional character Indiana Jones.

Against many logistical odds and financial challenges, Andrews began making plans for a museum-sponsored expedition. He took it upon himself to promote the idea to many of the well-to-do museum members who gave large amounts of money to science. Before too long, he was able to raise the amazing amount of a quarter million dollars—enough money

for Osborn to send him off on the adventure of a lifetime.[1]
Only Andrews thought that they had a good chance for success.
Later, he described their mission in these words:

> The main problem was to discover the geologic and pale-
> ontologic history of Central Asia; to find whether or not it
> had been the nursery of many of the dominant groups of
> animals, including the human race; and to reconstruct its
> past climate, vegetation and general physical conditions,
> particularly in relation to the evolution of man.[2]

He promoted the expedition to would-be backers as "the
largest undertaking in which the Museum has ever engaged
and will have far-reaching results, which should be of consid-
erable importance to our diplomatic and economic relations
with the Orient."[3]

Sometimes the most startling discoveries are made in science because of a single person's dedication to an idea. This
was to be the case with Andrews. For even though he never
found the remains of ancient humans in the Gobi, he led his
team to an astounding bounty of dinosaur fossils.

The Andrews Expeditions to Mongolia

The first expedition departed from New York City by ship,
took to land in Asia, and passed through the Great Wall of
China in April 1922. Andrews knew that they had to traverse
long expanses of desert, so he brought with him three Dodge
automobiles, two Fulton trucks, and a Chandler touring car
driven by the motorcade leader.[4] The cars and trucks were
used to transport the scientists as they explored the desert for

Roy Chapman Andrews and his Gobi Desert expedition team used camels to transport their supplies, including gasoline for the motor vehicles!

fossils. But what about supplies and fuel? There were no gasoline stations or grocery stores within days of their location. The answer was to add a regimen of camels to the expedition to transport their many supplies. This slower-moving caravan of seventy-five camels carried 400 gallons (1,500 liters) of gasoline, oil, and foodstuffs.[5] Most of the native Mongols had never seen automobiles before. There are no gas stations in the Gobi Desert, so the camel caravan traveled ahead with fuel and left it at points in the desert where the motor vehicles could refuel.

The automobiles were not exactly desert tested. Sandstorms soon scratched the windshields so severely that the drivers could no longer see through them. But for the most part, the cars and trucks were a rousing success, and the world's first motorized field expedition was under way.

Andrews brought several experts with him to explore inner Mongolia. Among them were two geologists to interpret the land formations and the age of the deposits. The chief paleontologist of the expedition, and second in command after Andrews, was the reliable Walter Granger. Granger was important to the success of the expedition because of his knowledge of fossils and how to dig them up properly. He certainly

One of the hazards of driving an automobile through the desert was getting stuck in the sand.

differed with Andrews about how best to excavate the delicate bones they found. Andrews recalled:

> Granger was pleased at our efforts to discover fossils but his approval ceased abruptly when it came to removing them. My favorite tool was a pick-ax, while he used a camel hair brush and a pointed instrument not much larger than a needle. When a valuable specimen had been discovered he would suggest that we go on a wild ass hunt, or anything that would take us as far as possible from the scene of his operations.[6]

Paleontologists Roy Chapman Andrews and Walter Granger investigate a fossil egg nest in Mongolia.

Granger is the same man who was digging mammal fossils in Egypt in 1907, prior to the arrival of Ernst Stromer and his German colleagues. Granger was also familiar with dinosaur fossils, having excavated many excellent specimens in western North America. The publicity before the expedition worried Granger, though. Andrews's promise of finding the origin of humankind was bold.

The first fossil bones discovered by the team were found in a region called Iren Dabasu. Although the hunters were searching for ancient man, they had found themselves at a fossil locality that was perhaps 100 million years older than the first humans. The pickings were scrappy, but they had found a few fragments of dinosaurs. It was not what they expected to find, but it was a delightful discovery nonetheless.

By the end of the summer of 1922, the field-weary team was briefly exploring a desolate basin of Cretaceous Period rocks. The area was bordered by a formation of majestic lava-capped, flat-topped hills and jutting rock sculptures that glowed red in the sharp-angled rays of the setting sun. They called the location Flaming Cliffs. In a hurry to leave the area before the harsh winter weather set in, the team had little time to explore the deposits. They picked up a few curious pieces of bone, including a small beaked skull that appeared to be that of a bird. They also found evidence of fossil eggshells, which they assumed were from prehistoric birds as well.

Before leaving for America, Andrews sent some of the fossils, including the skull, ahead to New York for examination. His colleagues in New York determined that the small skull was not that of a bird, but of a small horned dinosaur. It was a new horned dinosaur, older and smaller than its North American cousin *Triceratops*. It was given the name *Protoceratops*, "first horned face." Osborn sent them a telegram declaring, "You made a very important discovery. . . . Go back and get more."[7]

Andrews and his team returned to the fossil fields of Mongolia in 1923 and 1925. They first concen-

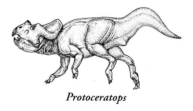

Protoceratops

trated on the area near Flaming Cliffs where the skull of *Protoceratops* had been found. Dinosaur bones were so plentiful there that they seemed to be finding a dinosaur under every bush.

Recovering more of *Protoceratops* was the first goal of the 1923 expedition. During two summers of work in 1923 and 1925, they found no fewer than a hundred specimens of this early horned dinosaur. Even more important than the number of specimens was that they represented many stages of growth of this dinosaur—a bonanza for a paleontologist. It is one of the most complete growth series ever discovered for any kind of dinosaur. The smallest specimens, barely out of the egg, showed a remarkable resemblance to their parents. The smallest skulls were only about 4 inches (10 centimeters) long. The frill that lined the back of the adult skull was but a ridge around the back of the neck until the dinosaur reached its adolescent years.

Protoceratops skull, as uncovered in the field.

Dinosaur Eggs

As thrilling as it was, the discovery of *Protoceratops* led to an even more astounding find that made headlines around the world. In 1923, soon after returning to the Flaming Cliffs region to look for more evidence of *Protoceratops,* one of the crew found a group of three fossil eggs. Granger was optimistic that these were dinosaur eggs and not those of birds because the fossil deposits were older than most known fossil birds. He rallied his team to sweep the area in search of more eggs. Before too long, eggs were found in many locations, some complete, some partially preserved, and some still lying intact in what appeared to be nests. They resembled the eggs of modern lizards, but larger. This was the first definitive discovery of dinosaur eggs in close association with dinosaur skeletons.

Andrews and Granger assumed that the eggs belonged to *Protoceratops*. Why else would they have been found with so many skeletons of baby *Protoceratops* all around? When they later found the remains of a meat eater on top of one of the nests, they reasoned that it was probably gobbling eggs and

This close-up photograph shows a nest of fossilized dinosaur eggs in Mongolia, 1925.

baby *Protoceratops*. They named the meat eater *Oviraptor*, or "egg thief." This theory held for nearly seventy years, until the American Museum sent a new team of paleontologists to explore the same area in Mongolia. They not only found some of the same kinds of eggs, but one of them contained an exquisitely preserved embryo of an unhatched dinosaur. To everyone's surprise, the dinosaur inside was not *Protoceratops*, but the predatory dinosaur *Oviraptor*.[8] This proved that the dinosaur once considered the hunter was actually the creator of the eggs. Such is the colorful and often unpredictable history of fossil dinosaur eggs. It seems that paleontologists should never count their eggs before they have seen an embryo inside.

Andrews and Granger found other new dinosaurs in Mongolia as well. The armored *Pinacosaurus* ("board lizard"), although small by armored dinosaur standards, was one of the largest creatures found at the site. It was about 12 feet (3.7 meters) long. They also discovered *Saurornithoides* ("birdlike lizard"), a predator measuring about 6.5 feet (2 meters), and the familiar *Velociraptor* ("swift thief"), a swift three-fingered meat eater that was about 6 feet (1.8 meters) long and had a sickle-claw on each foot.

Challenges of the Gobi

The dry, harsh physical conditions of Mongolia posed many unexpected challenges for the Central Asiatic Expedition. Andrews described one of the fierce sandstorms that threatened them in his most dramatic prose:

It came like a cyclone bringing a swirling red cloud of dust. In less than ten minutes the temperature dropped at least thirty degrees. A thousand shrieking demons seemed to be pelting my face with sand and gravel. . . . We could not see twenty feet, but we heard the clatter of tins, the sharp rip of canvas, and then a tumbled mass of camp beds, tables, chairs, bags, and pails swept down the hill. Lying flat on the ground with our faces buried in wet clothes we at least could breathe.[9]

Bandits were another unwanted distraction. Mongolia was torn by civil war, and there was little government control over the widespread territory. One Mongolian member of the expedition had been murdered during the winter following the first expedition. Andrews himself delighted in telling a story about his own encounter with brigands. He was driving one of the cars alone, scouting ahead of the party, when he was confronted by three Mongol bandits on horseback. As they drew their rifles to fire upon him, Andrews did the unexpected. Instead of fleeing, he drew his pistol and fired it wildly as he drove into the midst of the three horsemen. The horses were so startled that they bolted, taking their surprised and frightened riders with them. Andrews recalled the colorful story:

While the brigands were endeavoring to un-ship their rifles which were slung on their backs, their horses went into a wild series of leaps and bounds, bucking and rearing with fright, so that the men could hardly stay in their saddles.

When he last saw them, the bandits "were breaking all speed records on the other side of the valley."[10]

Roy Chapman Andrews with his Mongolian guide, Tserin.

Even though the expedition led by Roy Chapman Andrews never found evidence for the origin of human beings, they laid the groundwork for many exciting dinosaur and mammal discoveries that continue in Mongolia to this day. The American team was followed in 1946, 1947, and 1949 by a Russian expedition and then again by a combined Polish-Mongolian series of expeditions between 1963 and 1971. Between 1991 and 1995, the American Museum of Natural History returned to the area that Roy Chapman Andrews once traveled and continues to make periodic trips to explore the region.

CHAPTER 7

DINOSAURS OF THE AFRICAN SANDS

NEWLY DISCOVERED GIANTS OF AFRICA, 1995–2000

Question: What do the following fossil discoveries have in common?

- the world's largest crocodile
- the earliest meat-eating dinosaur
- a bizarre plant eater with 600 teeth
- a meat eater longer than *T. rex*
- a giant predatory dinosaur with a crocodile-like head
- a 70-foot- (21-meter-) long plant eater

Answer: They were all discovered on expeditions led by paleontologist Paul Sereno.

In the annals of modern paleontology, Paul Sereno must be considered a champion dinosaur hunter. Working from his base at the University of Chicago, this American scientist has had a tremendous knack for diving into challenging expeditions and coming away with startling new discoveries.

Although he teaches at the university, he seems most at home in the wilds of some far-flung land, hunting for elusive new dinosaur fossils. Many of his expeditions have taken him to rarely explored regions of the Southern Hemisphere, including South America and Africa.

Sereno: The Well-Traveled Paleontologist

Sereno led his first expedition at age thirty-one. He went to the foothills of the Andes mountains in Argentina, home of the fossil deposits dating from the earliest days of the dinosaurs. There he recovered the first complete remains of one of the earliest known dinosaurs—*Herrerasaurus* ("Herrera's lizard"). As if that were not enough, he returned in 1991 to discover an even more primitive meat-eating dinosaur called *Eoraptor* ("dawn thief"), a small creature that dated from the earliest days of the dinosaurs.

From there he was tempted to explore the northern reaches of Africa where the Sahara desert—and marauding, gun-toting rebels—posed serious risks to his team. One expedition needed an armed escort. The scientists stayed inside a walled compound at night, with guards posted in the surrounding fields to protect them.

In expeditions to Niger in 1993 and 1997 and to Morocco in 1995, Sereno and his teams discovered a new 27-foot (8-meter) predatory dinosaur, which they named *Afrovenator* ("African hunter"); an even larger predator, *Deltadromeus* ("delta runner"); and an exquisite skull of one of the largest meat eaters ever found: a specimen of *Carcharodontosaurus* ("shark-toothed lizard"). Originally named by famed German explorer Ernst Stromer in 1931, Sereno's new skull of *Carcharodontosaurus* had probably been attached to a body that was up to 45 feet (13.7 meters) long, 5 feet (1.5 meters) longer than *T. rex*. Other astounding finds included the 36-foot- (11-meter-) long *Suchomimus* ("crocodile mimic"), a peculiar fish-eating predator with a long snout like a crocodile; and the 70-foot- (21-meter-) long plant eater *Jobaria*, named for Jobar, a legendary North African creature.

Sereno's finds in Africa have told us much about the mysterious life of the Southern Hemisphere when the age of dinosaurs was coming to a close. Much was known about North American and Asian dinosaurs that lived at that same time, but little was known of their cousins on the other side of the world. It was a time when the land bridges that once connected the Northern and Southern Hemispheres were breaking apart, leaving dinosaurs from the north and the south to evolve in different ways. The discovery of *Jobaria*, for example, showed that some kinds of long-necked plant-eating giants still lived much as their ancestors had, even though these same kinds of dinosaurs had become extinct in North America by then.

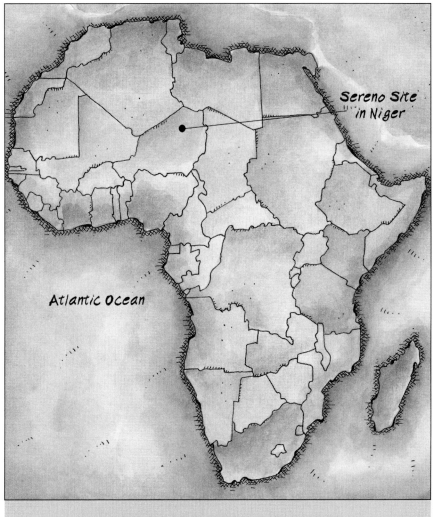

Sereno Site
in Niger

Atlantic Ocean

Paul Sereno traveled to Niger in 1993 and 1997.

The Biggest Expedition

Having made three previous trips to Africa, Sereno mounted his largest expedition ever in 2000. Returning to a more peaceful Niger, his expedition team consisted of fourteen students, professional paleontologists, and fossil-hunting enthusiasts. The entire trip lasted for 116 days, 96 of which were in the field digging dinosaurs and other fossils. The team even maintained a Web site from the field, where interested browsers could learn about daily discoveries, read messages from team members, and even see what was on the menu for dinner that night.

While having a Web site was considered innovative, the computer age could do nothing to make the back-breaking work of digging fossils any easier. In the desolate, sand-covered regions of the Sahara, Sereno's team used many of the same techniques for finding and digging fossils that had been perfected by his predecessors decades before. They carefully walked the fossil-bearing

Suchomimus is an African meat eater with a crocodile-like snout.

Jobaria was named in 1999 by paleontologist Paul Sereno.

areas looking for specimens, then set about the painstaking task of digging them up.

After several weeks of exploring, the work paid off in spectacular ways. A picture of Africa as it must have been about 110 million years ago began to emerge. The sand and stone yielded a wealth of fossil animals and even evidence of plants. A picture of a once temperate and teeming ecosystem became clearer. Sereno recalled how his expedition's discoveries brought the age of the dinosaurs back to life in their imaginations:

> Dinosaur bones clearly were plentiful throughout the region: the outcrop was a continuous stack of river-deposited sandstones. These rivers, many of which were broad, buried the animals that lived along their margins—like dinosaurs—as well as animals that actually lived in the rivers, like the crocodiles, turtles and fish.
>
> New river animals include small crabs and the teeth, bones and scales from many species of fish. We have found evidence of an enormous pterosaur—a flying reptile with a wingspan of 20 feet (6 and a half meters). Life on the banks of the rivers now includes a new large turtle with a domed shell that is more than one foot long. . . .
>
> We have found evidence of new plants as well. Greg Wilson, who is searching for the remains of the smallest animals including small mammals, found a handful of fossilized seeds measuring less than an inch long (about 2 centimeters).[1]

One of the prize catches of the 2000 expedition was not a dinosaur, but the largest crocodile specimen ever found. Called *Sarcosuchus* ("flesh crocodile"), it had been originally named by paleontologist Philippe Taquet in Niger in 1966. The new specimen reveals that this creature could grow to become a 40-foot- (12-meter-) long monster with a 5-foot (1.5-meter) jaw! In addition to the huge skull, Sereno's team found limb bones and large, foot-long armor plates from the

Paul Sereno and his fossil-hunting team discovered *Nigersaurus*, a long-necked plant-eating dinosaur. With up to 600 teeth, this dinosaur plucked leaves from branches. Here, it is having an unfortunate meeting with *Sarcosuchus*.

back of the creature. This giant croc was probably a dinosaur eater!

Fossils of dinosaurs and other creatures were found by the team as well. No fewer than four new small crocodiles were discovered along with the huge *Sarcosuchus*. The better part of the skeleton of the long-necked plant-eating dinosaur *Nigersaurus* ("Niger lizard") was also recovered. This bizarre creature had a mouth packed with as many as 600 slender teeth for plucking vegetation from branches.

In total, the 2000 expedition to Niger recovered five new predatory dinosaurs; five new plant-eating dinosaurs, including one with armor plating; six new crocodiles ranging in size from 40 feet (12 meters) long to less than 3 feet (0.9 meter); three new turtles; new fish and shelled invertebrates from the ancient riverbed; seeds; and mammal teeth.[2]

The bounty of fossils weighed 20 tons (18 metric tons). It was prepared for travel using 100 bags of plaster to make 274 protective fossil jackets.[3]

International fossil work brings with it a responsibility to the host country. Sereno's American team dug for fossils in Niger with permission of the government. Once the team in Chicago is finished studying the new specimens, the fossils will be returned to Niger for safekeeping and public display.

Paul Sereno's extraordinary Niger expedition in 2000 reminds us of the pioneers mentioned earlier in the book who first set foot in Africa in search of dinosaurs. It also informs us that the work of finding new dinosaurs is far from over.

CHAPTER 8

PATAGONIAN SURPRISE

TITANOSAURS AND BABIES IN SOUTH AMERICA, 1998–2001

While the most abundant dinosaur fossils have been found in North America and Asia, several regions below the equator have become the new frontiers of dinosaur science. Earlier chapters explored several expeditions to parts of North and East Africa. Here, we take a look at recent discoveries in Argentina, a South American nation with a rich fossil record of dinosaurs and other extinct creatures.

Argentina: Land of the Giants

Dinosaur discoveries are not new to Argentina. This country has been the location of many unusual dinosaur finds over the past hundred years. Most of these were in the desolate badlands of Patagonia, a vast expanse of inhospitable land stretching

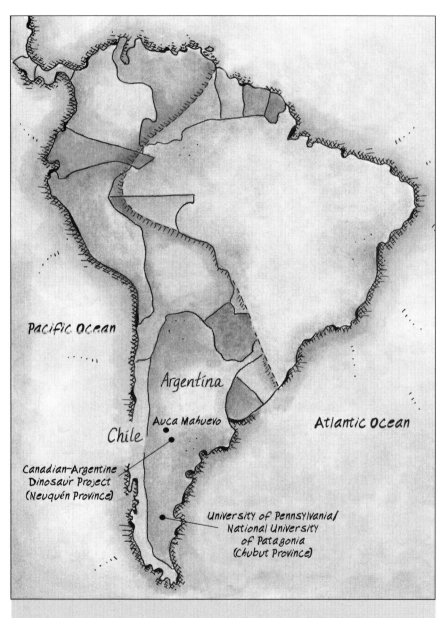

Southern South America is the site of record-breaking fossil finds.

down the western half of Argentina, encompassing the Andes mountains and parts of southern Chile.

The dinosaurs found in Argentina have a habit of breaking records. Argentina is currently the home of the oldest known dinosaurs (*Eoraptor* and *Herrerasaurus*), the largest meat-eating dinosaur (*Giganotosaurus,* "giant southern lizard"), and the biggest and bulkiest plant-eating dinosaur (*Argentinosaurus,* "Argentina lizard"). As if these distinctions were not enough, a recent discovery by a joint team from the United States and Argentina has uncovered a rare and remarkable fossil location: a vast dinosaur nesting ground where huge long-necked plant eaters once laid thousands of eggs.

Argentinosaurus (left) is attacked by *Gigantosaurus.*

This adventure began in 1997. A small expedition from the American Museum of Natural History was exploring a remote corner of northwestern Patagonia for evidence of fossil birds. The team was led by Luis Chiappe, an Argentine himself, and Lowell Dingus of the American Museum. Joining them from Argentina was Rodolfo Coria of the Carmen Funes Museum in Plaza Huincul. Coria is a skilled and conscientious paleontologist who finds himself in the middle of an extraordinary period of dinosaur discoveries in his native land. He led the teams that found and named *Argentinosaurus* and *Giganotosaurus*, the two biggest known dinosaurs. His base of

The fossil-hunting team is busy at a site in Patagonia.

operation is a humble little museum that has barely enough space to house these important discoveries. Scientists from around the world have begun to visit Coria's home turf, working alongside him and his team on many joint projects.

Dinosaur Nests–Everywhere!

The team from the American Museum of Natural History arrived in Patagonia for the purpose of searching for fossil bird remains. Instead, on only their second day in the field, they stumbled upon something entirely different. Driving through the badlands, they spotted a promising rock face in the distance. The area is mostly flat but distinguished by highly eroded mesas that rise above the plains like gigantic sand castles. These mesas often have cliffs and exposed layers of sediment that date from the days of the dinosaurs. The team spotted one of these cliffs and drove in its direction.

Having gone as far as they could in their truck, the paleontologists stopped and began to walk in the direction of the rock face. Before they got very far, however, they began to notice something strewn over the ground. There were fossil fragments all around them. Step by step, they were all beginning to find fossilized chunks of dinosaur eggs. Chiappe recalled:

> We realized that the entire place was virtually paved with these eggs and fragments of eggs. The concentration of eggs was so intense and rich that, in an area of roughly 100 yards by 200 yards, we counted about 195 clusters of eggs.[1]

Workers unearth clusters of dinosaur eggs in Patagonia.

Each cluster contained a half dozen or more eggs. Each egg was only about 5 or 6 inches (13 or 15 centimeters) in diameter and nearly round. The outside surface of the fossil egg fragments had a familiar pitted pattern seen before in dinosaur eggs. The scientists soon realized that they were walking through a vast fossilized nesting site of some kind of dinosaur. Dinosaur eggs are one of the rarest fossil discoveries, yet here they were surrounded by thousands of them. It was the discovery of a lifetime.

Rather than jumping for joy—and risk the accidental destruction of delicate egg fragments—the team immediately set to work collecting fossils. During the first short season, they recovered several excellent egg specimens and returned to the United States to examine them in a laboratory. In early 1998, Marilyn Fox, an expert at reconstructing fossil specimens, was carefully chipping inside one of the fossils when she discovered something extraordinary: tiny bones. The egg contained the fossilized remains of an unhatched dinosaur embryo. She hoped that enough of the tiny creature was intact so that it might reveal what kind of dinosaur had laid the egg.

After weeks of slow and painstaking preparation with the most delicate of hand tools, Fox could begin to surmise the dinosaur embryo's identity. It became clear that the tiny dinosaur embryo belonged to a family of some of the largest dinosaurs—the long-necked, plant-eating titanosaurs. The members of the embryo's family were probably between 40 and 60 feet (12 and 18 meters) long when fully grown. Titanosaurs had also been found throughout Africa, Europe, and India, all of which were connected at one time by land bridges.

To the delight of the scientists, not just one but many of the intact eggs and fragments contained fossilized pieces of embryonic titanosaurs. The team even recovered fossil skin casts, impressions of dinosaur skin—the first for any variety of embryonic dinosaur specimen. The skin pattern clearly showed reptilian scales. The embryonic titanosaurs measured about 12 inches (30 centimeters) long inside the egg.[2] That is amazingly small for a dinosaur that could one day be 60 feet (18 meters) long.

The site was given the clever name of Auca Mahuevo, combining a reference to an extinct volcano in the area named Auca Mahuida with the Spanish words *más huevos*, meaning "more eggs." The expedition team returned to the site for three more years. Each time Chiappe, Dingus, and Coria found more eggs and other surprises. Two large predatory dinosaurs are known to have frequented the site, including the 20-foot- (6-meter-) long *Aucasaurus* ("Auca lizard"). This newly discovered meat eater was a dangerous theropod about half the size of a fully grown titanosaur.[3] It probably roamed the perimeter of the adult titanosaur herd that gathered there, picking off weak members. This predator may have also ventured into the nesting area once the hatchlings began to emerge. The young titanosaurs, barely longer than a foot, would have been easy pickings for a large carnivore.

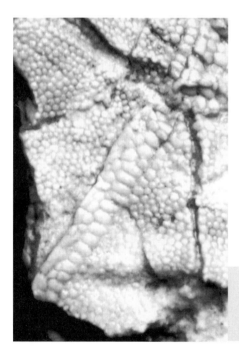

The team also brought geologic experts to help understand what had gone wrong 80 million years ago to bury the vast nesting ground. Using clues in the

Scientists were delighted to discover fossil skin impressions of titanosaur embryos.

soil and rock, the telltale signs of a natural disaster emerged. It appears that a flood washed over the site and buried thousands of dinosaur nests in mud.[4]

Scientists also concluded that the same nesting site had been used repeatedly, possibly for many successive breeding seasons. They discovered at least four layers of egg sites on different geologic levels, meaning each layer had been laid at a separate time. A picture of the days of these dinosaurs was further completed by the discovery of multiple tracks of sauropod footprints near the site. This confirmed scientists' theory that the titanosaurs traveled in herds.

The magnitude of the Patagonian egg site is so extensive that Coria believes it will take many years to fully explore. He calls the site "unique," a once-in-a-lifetime opportunity to study the entire ecosystem of these dinosaurs. The area not only includes fossils of the titanosaurs and their eggs, but of ancient plant life and other creatures, including other dinosaurs, that lived in the same area with them.[5]

✦ ✦ ✦

Hunting Dinosaurs in Patagonia

An Author's Account

Author Thom Holmes recently dug for dinosaurs in Patagonia with two different research expeditions. This is his account of what it is like to camp in the wilderness and discover dinosaur bones.

Neuquén Province, Patagonia, Argentina, 1999

There are no trees in Patagonia. That's the first thing I noticed on my first adventure to Argentina to dig dinosaurs. The earth is parched and the vegetation barely covers the ground. The days of early autumn are still hot—often approaching 100 degrees Fahrenheit (34 degrees Celsuis). But at night we needed warm sleeping blankets, as the temperature dipped below freezing. We slept in tents, cooked and ate meals around a campfire, and went to sleep early to conserve our energy for the next day's work.

On my first trip to Patagonia I worked as a member of a crew for the Canadian-Argentine Dinosaur Project. Headed jointly by Phil Currie of the Royal Tyrrell Museum of Palaeontology (Alberta, Canada), and Rodolfo Coria of the Carmen Funes Museum (Plaza Huincul, Argentina), we were working on a significant discovery. It was a bone bed of a half dozen large predatory dinosaurs. They had apparently died while traveling in a pack, a revelation that contradicts the old idea that meat eaters traveled alone. This yet-unnamed kind of dinosaur is new to science and may one day be recognized as the largest meat eater of them all.

Just how many individual dinosaur skeletons were buried at the site was not known until late in the expedition. The first week was spent chipping away with shovels, picks, chisels, and hammers at the massive amount of rock—called overburden—that still covered most of the site. We estimated that we had removed about 20 tons of rock by the time we were done—enough to fill a few small trucks. All of this was done using hand tools and plastic buckets to carry the rock to a waste pile.

Heavy rains set in after a few days, making the experience even more challenging. The camp was separated from the fossil site by a rut about twenty feet deep whose sides became slippery with

Author Thom Holmes on a recent dinosaur dig in Patagonia

water and mud. We crossed the gorge each day to get to the fossil site, hugging the muddy sides so as not to slip or fall. Phil and Rodolfo helped rig a tarp over the dig site to protect it—and us— from the driving rain that persisted for several days.

When it wasn't raining, the sun beat down on us without mercy. It is said that the earth's protective ozone layer is not as dense over the lower regions of the Southern Hemisphere, where we were. Without this protective layer, one becomes highly susceptible to sunburn due to the penetrating ultraviolet rays of the sun. One day on the dig I asked Rodolfo if they had any problems with the ozone layer. In his characteristic manner, he jokingly remarked, "We don't have problems with it because we don't have an ozone layer!" I put on more sunscreen after that.

Phil Currie was the first one to find the hint of a new bone layer. After that, we all dug in and worked the site with smaller tools so as not to damage any bones. After several more weeks, the expedition recovered hundreds of bones of several dinosaurs, all jumbled together as if they had died in a pile. There was evidence of a river channel running through the site. It is possible that they died on the banks of a shallow river—for reasons unknown—and were then buried by mud from a sudden flood of water rushing downstream.

Chubut Province, Patagonia, Argentina, 2000

Another expedition to Patagonia took me to Chubut Province to dig dinosaurs with scientists from the University of Pennsylvania and the National University of Patagonia. The American team included noted American dinosaur expert Peter Dodson and then-graduate students Matt Lamanna and Josh Smith. Our Argentine host was Rubén Martinez.

This was a smaller group than my previous expedition with Currie and Coria. We cooked dinner from the tailgate of a truck set up at the campsite and then sat inside to eat, sipping soup and eating stew, as the temperatures dropped quickly at night.

The dig site in Chubut was more than a mile from the camp-site because it was impossible to drive any closer. It was a daily challenge just getting to and from the site. The landscape was hilly and precarious, with highly eroded mesas rising all around us. Every morning, we hiked over this rugged terrain with all of the equipment and water needed for a day's work. We left soon after sunrise and returned as the sun went down. Once at the site, we hovered over a bone bed containing a wide assortment of never-before-known dinosaurs. There was evidence of meat eaters and large long-necked plant eaters. One meat eater is closely related to a sizable predator called Megaraptor. All of these are being studied at this time so that the dinosaurs can be properly named and described.

When you work in the sun all day, you begin to acquire a knack for finding a shady place to rest. Without any trees, we often found ourselves huddling behind a rock wall or in a crevasse where the sun could not beat down directly on us.

The area surrounding this dig was littered with loose bones. These had been buried in rock at one time but were revealed through the natural forces of erosion. Most were just "spare parts," as Dodson calls them—and of little scientific value because they were loose and unconnected to other bones or evidence. Some had probably been sitting unprotected for decades—maybe even hundreds of years. The power of wind and rain and sand had made some of these surface fossils shine like jewels.

The thrill of finding a dinosaur fossil is difficult to describe. Some of the most exciting finds are often the smallest and easily overlooked unless one is looking closely and digging carefully. We found several small meat-eater teeth in this way. It is a thrill to realize that these artifacts of once-living creatures had not seen the light of day for over 80 million years.

By the end of this expedition, the weather had turned quite cold and snow was beginning to fall. The fossils themselves were too far away from the camp to be carried back by hand, so a helicopter was brought in to lift them out and get them to a truck.

The Patagonian badlands of Argentina remain one of the most remote and exciting frontiers of dinosaur science. It is one of those places where nearly every dinosaur that is discovered is different from others discovered before. Although the work is hard, it is paradise for a paleontologist.

The Search Continues

Every dinosaur fossil seen in a museum has a rich history of discovery. Digging dinosaurs can be a difficult task. Men and women who search for dinosaurs sometimes face harsh weather conditions and geologic challenges that make their work difficult and sometimes risky.

As shown in these pages, dinosaurs have been found in many parts of the world. While North America and China are known for having the most dinosaur fossils, many other parts of the world are revealing new and unusual fossils as well. Argentina and North Africa are two current hot spots where new discoveries are made every year.

Dinosaurs continue to be discovered at an amazing rate. There are many more to be found. Perhaps one day you will find some dinosaur that has never been seen before.

CHAPTER NOTES

Chapter 2. The Dinosaur Bone Rush in America

1. Charles Schuchert, *O. C. Marsh: Pioneer in Paleontology* (New Haven, Conn.: Yale University Press, 1940), p. 100.

2. Ibid., p. 191.

3. Ibid., p. 193.

4. Ibid., pp. 196–197.

5. John H. Ostrom and John S. McIntosh, *Marsh's Dinosaurs* (New Haven, Conn.: Yale University Press, 1966), p. 29.

6. Holmes, pp. 121–123.

Chapter 3. A Dinosaur Safari in Africa

1. David E. Fastovsky and David B. Weishampel, *The Evolution and Extinction of the Dinosaurs* (New York: Cambridge University Press, 1996), p. 235.

2. Edwin H. Colbert, *Men and Dinosaurs* (New York: E. P. Dutton, 1968), pp. 244–245.

3. Ibid., p. 248.

Chapter 4. The Lost and Found Dinosaurs of Egypt

1. Walter Granger, *Faiyum Diary*. Copyright © by Vincent L. Morgan for The Granger Papers Project. <http://users.rcn.com/granger.nh.ultranet/FaiyumCover.html> (November 12, 2002).

2. Ibid.

3. Ibid.

4. William Nothdurft and Josh Smith, *The Lost Dinosaurs of Egypt* (New York: Random House, 2002), pp. 19–20.

5. John Prendergast, *The Pennsylvania Gazette* (Philadelphia: University of Pennsylvania, July/August 2001), <http://www.upenn.edu/gazette/0701/prendergast.html> (November 12, 2002).

Chapter 5: The Canadian Dinosaur Bone Rush

1. Edwin H. Colbert, *Men and Dinosaurs* (New York: E. P. Dutton, 1968), p. 188.

2. Barnum Brown, *Field Book 1910,* collection of the American Museum of Natural History (New York), <http://paleo.amnh.org/field/brown1908-11/04.html> (November 12, 2002).

3. Katherine Rogers, *A Dinosaur Dynasty* (Missoula, Mont.: Mountain Press Publishing Co, 1991), p. 151.

Chapter 6: The Discovery of Dinosaur Eggs

1. David A. E. Spalding, *Dinosaur Hunters* (Rocklin, Calif.: Prima Publishing, 1993), p. 215.

2. Edwin H. Colbert, *Men and Dinosaurs* (New York: E. P. Dutton, 1968), p. 204.

3. V. L. Morgan and S. G. Lucas, "Walter Granger, 1872–1941, Paleontologist" *New Mexico Museum of Natural History and Science Bulletin 19,* 2002, p. 31.

4. Ibid., p. 26.

5. Spalding, p. 216.

6. Mark A. Norell, Eugene S. Gaffney, and Lowell Dingus, *Discovering Dinosaurs in the American Museum of Natural History* (New York: Alfred A. Knopf, 1995), p. 196.

7. Spalding, p. 218.

8. Mark A. Norell, J. M. Clark, D. Dashzeveg, R. Barsbold, Luis M. Chiappe, A. R. Davidson, M. C. McKenna, A. Perle, and Michael J. Novacek, "A Theropod Dinosaur Embryo and the Affinities of the Flaming Cliffs Dinosaur Eggs," *Science,* vol. 266, pp. 779–782.

9. Spalding, p. 212.

10. Joseph Wallace, *The American Museum of Natural History's Book of Dinosaurs and Other Ancient Creatures* (New York: Simon & Schuster, 1994), p. 57.

Chapter 7: Dinosaurs of the African Sands

1. Paul Sereno, Project Exploration, 2000, <http://www.projectexploration.org/niger2000/10_03_2000.htm> (November 12, 2002).

2. Ibid.

3. Ibid.

Chapter 8: Patagonian Surprise

1. Luis M. Chiappe, *The Discovery*, American Museum of Natural History, 1998, <http://www.amnh.org/exhibitions/expeditions/dinosaur/patagonia/index.html> (November 12, 2002).

2. Luis M. Chiappe and Lowell Dingus, *Walking on Eggs* (New York: Scribner, 2001), p. 173.

3. Ibid., p. 180.

4. Luis M. Chiappe, "Dinosaur Embryos," *National Geographic*, December 1998, pp. 34–41.

5. Author conversation with Rodolfo Coria, March 1999.

GLOSSARY

anatomy—The science of the structure of plants and animals.

badlands—A dry, barren region of land with highly eroded land features and little vegetation. These areas often have large exposures of rocks with fossils in them.

ceratopsian—"Horned face." A member of the group of horned dinosaurs including the psittacosaurs, protoceratopsids, and ceratopsids.

clutch—A group of eggs in a nest.

Cretaceous Period—The third and final major time division (144 to 65 million years ago) of the Mesozoic Era. The end of the age of dinosaurs.

dysentery—A disease of the intestine, usually caused by an infection. Severe and sometimes bloody diarrhea are symptoms of dysentery.

ecosystem—A community of animals and plants and the environment in which they live.

embryo—A vertebrate organism while it is still in its egg.

evolution—The patterns of change through time of living organisms.

fauna—Animal life.

field season—A period during which a paleontologist works outside digging fossils.

fossil jacket—A hard coating consisting of cloth strips soaked in plaster of paris that is applied to the outside of a fossil to protect it from damage. Fossil jackets are usually applied to a fossil while it is still in the ground, prior to attempting to lift, move, or transport it.

hatchling—A newly hatched dinosaur or bird.

Jurassic Period—The second of the three major time divisions (208 to 144 million years ago) of the Mesozoic Era.

Mesozoic Era—The time of the dinosaurs (245 to 65 million years ago).

outcrop—An exposure of sedimentary rock, often containing fossils.

overburden—Rock and dirt that lies above or on top of a deposit of fossils in sedimentary rock, and which must be removed before the fossils can be excavated.

paleontology—The study of life-forms of the geologic past, especially through the analysis of plant and animal fossils.

predator—A meat-eating creature.

sauropod—Any of the large plant-eating saurischian dinosaurs with long necks and long tails.

sedimentary rocks—Rocks in which fossils are found. They gradually form, layer by layer, on the surface of the earth from the breakdown by erosion of older rocks.

skin impressions—A fossilized pressing or cast of skin that was once made in the mud and preserved through geologic forces. The actual skin is no longer present; only its impression remains.

specimen—The fossil bones of a single individual creature. More than one specimen of the same genus and species of an extinct creature may be found.

theropod—Any of the group of meat-eating dinosaurs, all of which walked on two legs.

Triassic Period—The first of the three major time divisions (245 to 208 million years ago) of the Mesozoic Era.

FURTHER READING

Chiappe, Luis M., and Lowell Dingus. *Walking on Eggs*. New York: Scribner, 2001.

Farlow, James Orville. *Bringing Dinosaur Bones to Life: How Do We Know What Dinosaurs Were Really Like?* Danbury, Conn.: Franklin Watts, 2001.

Nothdurft, William, and Josh Smith. *The Lost Dinosaurs of Egypt*. New York: Random House, Inc., 2002.

Novacek, Michael. *Dinosaurs of the Flaming Cliffs*. New York: Doubleday, 1996.

Internet Addresses

American Museum of Natural History, *Fossil Halls*, n.d., <http://www.amnh.org/exhibitions/permanent/fossils/>

National Geographic Society, *Dinosaur Eggs*, n.d., <www.nationalgeographic.com/dinoeggs/>

Russ Jacobson, *Dino Russ's Lair: Dinosaur and Vertebrate Paleontology Information*, n.d., <http://www.isgs.uiuc.edu/dinos/dinos_home.html>

INDEX